ATTRACTING GARDEN
POLLINATORS

This book is dedicated to my Dad, Max, who always towered above, but treasured the little things in life. A giant, fluffy bumblebee reunited with his beautiful flower at last.

ATTRACTING GARDEN
POLLINATORS

JEAN VERNON

WHITE OWL
AN IMPRINT OF PEN & SWORD BOOKS LTD.
YORKSHIRE – PHILADELPHIA

First published in Great Britain in 2022 by
Pen and Sword WHITE OWL
An imprint of
Pen & Sword Books Ltd
Yorkshire - Philadelphia

ISBN 978 1 52671 190 8

A CIP catalogue record for this book is available from the British Library.

Typeset in 11/14 pts Cormorant Infant
by SJmagic DESIGN SERVICES, India.

Printed and bound in India by Replika Press Pvt. Ltd.

Pen & Sword Books Ltd incorporates the imprints of Pen & Sword Books Archaeology, Atlas, Aviation, Battleground, Discovery, Family History, History, Maritime, Military, Naval, Politics, Railways, Select, Transport, True Crime, Fiction, Frontline Books, Leo Cooper, Praetorian Press, Seaforth Publishing, Wharncliffe and White Owl.

For a complete list of Pen & Sword titles please contact

PEN & SWORD BOOKS LIMITED
47 Church Street, Barnsley, South Yorkshire, S70 2AS, England
E-mail: enquiries@pen-and-sword.co.uk
Website: www.pen-and-sword.co.uk

or

PEN AND SWORD BOOKS
1950 Lawrence Rd, Havertown, PA 19083, USA
E-mail: Uspen-and-sword@casematepublishers.com
Website: www.penandswordbooks.com

Contents

Introduction

The interconnectedness of life never fails to amaze me. I am fascinated by the way that the animal and plant kingdom interact, the incredible evolutionary traits that plants use to attract insects and the remarkable ways that insects and other pollinators utilise plants to fuel their lifestyle and augment their survival. It's not just that plants need pollinators to reproduce, it's also about how the right pollinator can perform such a delicate role, probably totally unaware of the chain of reactions that it starts as it feeds on the flowers.

In nature we observe all manner of intricate and fragile relationships between predators and prey as well as plants and pollinators. Often these are the results of millennia of evolution, with the plants evolving alongside the pollinators that seek out their pollen and nectar. And yet our gardens are not natural. They are the canvas of painters whose paint pallete is plants, whose inspiration is magazines and flower shows and whose brushes are trowels and forks. Quite often these gardens, our personal pride and joy, are packed full of plants from all over the world, rubbing leaves and stems with each other in new combinations and with unexpected consequences.

Gardeners have stopped nature in her tracks to manipulate, embellish and dramatise a patch until it is full to bursting with plants from far distant shores mixed in with natives and embellished with pots and planters of fabulous flamboyant flowers and foliage.

Despite this, our gardens are made up of layer upon layer of interconnected and fragile relationships. It's an entangled web of life so complicated and at times so brutal that it would make a soap opera look tame. And yet it's quite magical too. Left to her own devices nature always rebalances and overcomes challenges in unexpected but often very efficient ways. While man seems intent on poisoning the planet and milking every last resource from her grips, nature finds a way to rise to the challenge.

But gardens and urban plots, be they small scale, large or allotments, are hot spots of pollinator diversity and abundance (Ref 1). Recent research from Bristol University has highlighted the importance of our gardens for pollinator survival (Ref 2). And as the pandemic rolls on the importance of homegrown food and immersing ourselves in nature for our physical and mental health has become all too clear. Just like the pollinators, we crave and need a rich diversity of flowering plants.

Gardens small or large, modern or cottage or wild have the potential to support garden pollinators. © JeanVernon/HamptonCourtFlowerShow2017/ColourBoxGarden/Charlie Bloom/Simon Webster.

Pollinator Heroes

Insects are everywhere, present in every environment known to man in quantities and a diversity that is hard to visualise. And yet generally we dismiss them, ignore them and rarely appreciate the vital role that they play in nature. Some people find them repulsive, others regard them as pests or plagues, and rarely do we look deeper at their inherent beauty or relate to them and their important roles in our lives. Insects are virtual aliens but without them human life as we know it would either not exist at all, or would be completely and totally different.

Every dimension of our world is rich in insect life; they are the most abundant creatures on earth and yet they are rarely revered and often badly understood.

Peer a little closer and you will discover that these creatures have beautiful faces, a caring/nurturing nature and really fascinating lives. Pollinators are the charismatic elephants and fluffy tigers of the insect world and need our attention and respect more than ever.

Pollinators are all around us. Here three species share the flower head of one plant. © Lance Featherstone.

If you still struggle to fall in love with insects, then pledge to make an exception and join me in my quest to bring the world of pollinators to your attention. These are mostly insects and it's time that their incredible contribution to our world, our gardens and our food was put firmly into the light. Without our precious pollinators we would be in serious trouble and as gardeners we can make huge differences to their survival, existence and lives. Now is the time to really step up and take a closer look at insects, starting with pollinators.

Let me take you on a journey to explore some of the incredible insects that work for us; they are exploited, underpaid and generally underappreciated, but these little creatures are so important that they need a fresh campaign to tell everyone about them, before it is too late.

ATTRACTING GARDEN POLLINATORS

CHAPTER ONE

What is a Pollinator?

We take pollinators for granted. And yet these are the creatures that live alongside us, within nature and the landscapes and gardens that we have created or even sometimes destroyed. We don't always see them, we exploit them, and sometimes we kill them, but without their help we would surely starve. For not only do they pick up and deliver pollen to the plants we need for food, but they also ensure that the cattle and livestock are fed, that we have seed to sow and that our cupboards, fridges and fruit bowls are full of nuts, seeds, fruits and vegetables.

Pollinators live their lives adjusting to the pressures that we have created in their world, navigating the landscape changes we have carved on their habitats and feeding on the plants that we allow to grow.

Scientists frequently research and study these fascinating creatures. Quite incredibly some engineers believe that they can create miniature robot pollinators or pollinating techniques that will replace this essential role. They have an apparent misunderstanding of the incredible complexities that exist in the intimate relationships between plants and pollinators and the fragile knife-edge that these precious creatures balance upon.

In the UK at least, pollinators are generally insects. But across the world all manner of birds, bats, mice and even possums also play similar roles. While pollinators probably don't realise they are performing this very vital role, the act of pollination is not a hit-and-miss event. Each plant species has a very unique pollen that is needed to fertilise its seed. Pollen from other species will not work. So they have evolved ways to make pollination more likely, more effective and more abundant. The actual delivery of pollen is a bit like sending a letter in the post: it needs the correct address and postcode to get to the right person. It's the same with plants and pollen, but the vector, the pollinator (like the postman) has to collect the right pollen and deliver it to the right place. Most plants need cross-pollination, so it is also very important is that pollen from one plant is taken to another of the same species to ensure that cross-pollination occurs. This combines the genes of two different plants, increases the gene pool and creates stronger offspring that are not inbred. Though plants can't actively move around to find a mate they can and do play a part in the rituals between themselves and their pollinators. They do this by timing when their flowers open, increasing or decreasing their nectar offering, and some even have flowers that change colour when pollinated. (Ref 3).

Many pollinators visit flowers for their pollen. It's a protein rich food that some insects use to feed their young. Most will also feed on nectar or collect nectar to store for energy, share with nest mates or provision a brood cell as a food source. Just because an insect visits a flower doesn't make it a pollinator. But many will pick up pollen on their bodies as they wait for a mate, feed on nectar or actively collect pollen. The effectiveness of a pollinator is dependent on several factors such as its abundance, how hairy it is, its behaviour, the size of its body and how often it visits flowers. (Ref 3). While the size of the pollinator usually corresponds to the amount of pollen it can pick up, what is just as important is that the body of the pollinator can span the distance between the male (anthers) and female (stigma) parts of the flower to effect pollination (Ref 3).

What's so Great About Pollen?

Pollen is gold dust for so many reasons. If you suffer from hay fever you might not agree, but honestly, without pollen we would all be in trouble.

Pollen is rich in protein. For plants it is the male 'sperm' that carries the genetic information of a plant. In order for it to actually make a seed, it needs to merge with a female ovule inside the plant ovary. Once a correct pollen grain is presented to the plant stigma it grows a tube down into the ovule and delivers its genetic information.

The sum of the pollen from one plant with the ovule of another creates a seed that shares characteristics from both parent plants. It is this cross-pollination that introduces genes from other plant populations and leads to stronger plants and a bigger genetic pool. These are the basics of how plants change, survive, improve and evolve.

Pollen grains are completely unique to the species of plants that create them and only very rarely can a hybrid be created between two different plant species.

For pollinators the pollen protein is a valuable food.

Every grain of pollen has a different shape depending on the plant species. © JeanVernon/BBKA exhibit.

What do Pollinators Need?

The first thing that pollinators need is nectar. At times nectar is more important than pollen because it is an energy source, a bit like a sugar rush, and fuels their daily activity. The nectar attracts the pollinators to the flower for their sugar hit. Some pollinators use the flowers as a meeting place, a bit like a pub where the males can feed, meet and check out the 'girls'. It's a clever move because the females of their species will visit the same sort of flowers to feed, so it's a good place for speed dating.

Pollinators need a food supply from the time that they emerge from 'hibernation' as adults, until they have successfully mated and laid their eggs. Most pollinators have a short life cycle and spend a lot of their lives as egg, larva, pre-pupa or pupa. It is the adult, winged stage of life when they can fly between plants and flowers and not only feed themselves on nectar, but also collect food for the next generation. And that's where the pollen comes in. While many pollinators pick up pollen on their bodies as they feed on nectar, others, like the bees, actively collect it as a protein-rich material with which to feed their young. Some pollinators, like the wasps, collect live protein-rich prey to feed their offspring, while others, like the butterflies and moths, feed up as caterpillars and simply supplement their diet with nectar to fuel their movement as adults.

Pollinators also need somewhere to nest or lay their eggs and different insects have different needs. Butterflies and moths need the correct plants for their caterpillars to feed on. Solitary bees might favour the hollow stems of garden perennials to make a nest. Our gardens provide very important and very varied habitats for our pollinators to shelter, breed, nest and overwinter.

Nectar

Nectar is basically insect 'click bait'; it is the sugar rich super food that they need to support their activity. Most adult pollinators need a copious amount of nectar to fuel their lifestyle and it needs to be accessible and present at the right time in their lifecycle. That means flowers. But this is where it gets clever. Plants don't produce nectar for their own needs; they make it to attract pollinating insects.

Nectar is usually positioned at the base of the flower, luring the pollinator insect inside for its rich reward, but in the process the pollinator picks up pollen on its body and takes it to the next flower when it moves on. This facilitates pollination, giving the nectar a starring role in procedures.

The flowers need the pollinators at the right time in their lifecycle to move the pollen from plant to plant, so the plant has to produce the nectar rich flowers when their perfect pollinator is looking for food. The flowers are flags waving in the breeze to passing pollinators, shouting their wares and advertising their open nectar bars and diners to the energy hungry insects. Nectar is food for the adults. Though sometimes pollen is wetted with nectar to provide some additional energy for the developing larvae.

Quality of nectar varies considerably, and it may contain flower essences that could offer healing properties to the feeding insects, or pesticide residues if the plants have been treated with toxic chemicals. Some plants replenish their nectaries faster than others. Borage and echium, for example, replace the nectar regularly, making them popular nectar bars. Environmental factors also come into play. The weather affects when a plant comes in to flowers. A dry spell may require a plant to sacrifice the nectar supply to survive a drought. Climate change can affect the flowering times of many spring flowers, creating a lack of food for pollinators when they need it the most. Gardeners can manipulate flower forage by forcing things to flower earlier, holding plants back to extend the season, sowing earlier and later crops and doing the 'Chelsea Chop'.

Gardens for Pollinators

Our gardens have a vital role in ensuring the survival of many pollinator species. As garden guardians we have the power to really make a difference. You don't have to

Beautiful borders are not out of bounds when you plant for pollinators. This textured mix of Ammi majus, veronicastrum, alliums, cornflowers, verbena, scabious creates a soft and beautiful dreamscape for pollinators and people. © JeanVernon/HamptonCourtFlowerShow2018/ Apeiron: The Dibond Garden/Alex Rainford-Roberts.

have a garden designed for pollinators to attract them, but you can hugely increase the biodiversity on your plot by changing a few of your gardening techniques. We don't have to do much to attract these creatures onto our plot; the simple act of growing flowering plants is a magnet for many species. But there is so much more we can do to ensure their safe existence.

Flower Shapes

Common advice for gardeners is to grow plants that flower right through the year. The critical times are late winter into early spring and late summer into autumn. While we might have a few snowdrops that blur the margin between winter and spring that is not enough to support the diversity of pollinators emerging from their winter rest. They need much more. But it's not just essential to ensure there are things in flower. Every pollinator species has different needs and in particular different tongue lengths, which dictates how they feed.

When you consider that plants and their pollinators evolved together and that many of the beautiful plants we grow in our gardens are not only highly bred to look flamboyant, but may also hail from far distant shores thousands of miles from their pollinator partners, you start to understand the difficulties that our pollinators face. Nectar quality varies but if an insect can reach it and it's the best around at that time, then it becomes a good source of food. The origin of the plant is not important. It's the ease of access to the rewards on offer, namely the pollen and nectar that matters. (Ref 4). Throughout this book you will find mentions of plants for different pollinators, some with photos of pollinators feeding, and there's a whole chapter of even more plants towards the back. You don't need to be a botanist to understand any of this. There are simple ways to help and attract your garden pollinators.

Some pollinators like butterflies have long tongues. Comma butterfly on lavender. © Martin Mulchinock.

Floral Diners

Think about the flower shapes in your garden. The diversity is spellbinding and helps gardeners to create a tapestry of texture, colour and even fragrance in the borders. But if you've got a very short tongue like a hoverfly, wasp, fly, honeybee, or some of the bumblebees like the White-tailed bumblebee or the Buff-tailed bumblebee you can't reach the nectaries deep inside tubular flowers (but some do cheat!). Instead you need landing pad flowers like the daisies, or the carrot family or even the thistles and dandelions. While some of these names may conjure horror in many gardeners remember that in every plant family there are garden-worthy members and that even the weeds, shock horror, are really important food sources. And of course it's not just about nectar. Many of our pollinators need pollen, so open flowers with easy access make eating or gathering pollen easier.

For simplicity we can split the flower shapes into different forms and look at access to the pollen and nectar. The big no-no when choosing flowers for pollinators are the double flowered, frilly, highly bred types, which have sometimes forfeited nectaries for extra petals. Great for the flower show perhaps but best avoided if space is tight and you want to do the best for garden pollinators.

Cup-Shaped Flowers

Most pollinators can climb into cup or bowl-shaped flowers to access the pollen and nectar. The flowers can also provide an overnight shelter for some insects. Great plants to choose for early spring are crocus and hellebores. Others include campanulas, poppies and tulips.

Open flowers like this poppy are perfect for short tongued pollinators. © Jean Vernon.

Clusters of Little Flowers

Lots of flowers in one place make a great fast food station for pollinators. This is especially important in spring when these insects need plenty of food quickly. It's an efficient way for them to feed and if they don't have to travel too far to get sustenance, even better. Great plants for early spring include the grape hyacinths and the flowering currants. These are suitable for short and medium-tongued pollinators. But hebes, lavender, buddleia, scabious and eryngiums are also particularly good for summer dining.

Flower spikes with lots of flowers in one place provide fast food for pollinators. Volucella inanis on hebe. © Jean Vernon.

Frilly Landing Pads

The light and airy frilly flowering pads of the carrot family are fantastic food plants for short-tongued pollinators like the wasps, hoverflies and other flies. They won't all take the weight of big bumblebees but are a beautiful addition to the border. Plants like dill, fennel, angelica, *Ammi majus* and Queen Anne's lace are all lovely plants for the garden. But hogweed, wild carrot and the other umbellifers are also important pollinator plants.

Pea Flowers

The flowers of the pea family are a little more complicated for a pollinator to navigate; it has to virtually push its way in to get to the nectar, which demands a bit of strength and a determined insect. Small vetch flowers are easier and different species visit depending on whether they can access the flowers. For example shorter-tongued pollinators visit the white clover, but only the longer tongued species can reach the nectar in red clover. In my garden the perennial sweet peas are a magnet for Leaf-cutter bees. Many of the larger pea flowers, like coronilla, lupins, sweet peas and even runner beans are excellent flowers for the longer-tongued pollinators like butterflies, moths and some of the bumblebee species like the Common Carder bee.

Pollinators need to be large enough or strong enough to access pollen and nectar from pea flowers. Bombus pascuorum on perennial sweet pea. © Jean Vernon.

Hooded Flowers

Some flowers like those of the dead nettles and salvias have hooded flowers that the pollinators either climb into or poke their tongues into for the rich pot of nectar. These flowers are best suited to longer-tongued pollinators such as some of the bumblebees or the hovering, long-tongued Hawk moths. However, the sweet reward attracts nectar robbers. Some of the short-tongued bumblebees can't sup from these flowers so instead chew holes directly above the nectary to poke their tongues through. These also provide access for secondary robbers like honeybees to steal the nectar too.

Long tubular flowers like salvias need a long tongue to access the nectar, unless they have been plundered by short tongued nectar robbers. Look closely and you can see the holes this honeybee is feeding from. © Jean Vernon.

Daisy Flowers

If you had to design the perfect flower for most pollinators it would probably look like a daisy. The central cone is made up of many tiny florets, each one rich in nectar and pollen. The petals are like flags pointing towards the dinner plate of food, and the strong daisy stems can support the weight of the feeding insects. There are lots of fabulous daisy flowers that you can grow for garden pollinators. Good ones to choose are asters, cone flowers (echinacea), dahlias, heleniums, rudbeckia, cosmos and marguerites.

In built up areas it is the presence of gardens, waste ground and even road verges and roundabouts that support these precious creatures, and yet if we joined each patch together like a giant virtual jigsaw, the area of just our private gardens alone would in effect be a vast 270,000 hectare nature reserve. Each and every garden can make a difference. And more importantly every gardener can help spread the word and lead by example, sharing not only plants and seeds but advice and knowledge about these unsung heroes of nature.

To help our pollinators we need to start with our gardens and work outwards. We need to join our gardens together with safe corridors of plants where they can forage and move between garden oases safely. We need to scrutinise our gardens, what we grow and the way that we garden and make bold decisions for all pollinators.

Daisy flowers are virtual dinner plates for our pollinating friends. Hoverfly (Syrphus spp) on daisy. © Jean Vernon.

For them to prosper and thrive we need to set our own garden rules, be aware of the dangers facing mini-beasts of all types and have a future-proof plan for all pollinators and wildlife.

Most of all we need an understanding of their lifecycle, their needs and their quirky behaviour so that we can keep them safe and share the beauty and idiosyncrasies of bees and pollinators with others, and spread the love.

Wildlife Corridors – Joining Everything Together

Nature doesn't understand, respect or even notice the boundaries we have tattooed on the countryside. But, the restrictive fences and walls that delineate our gardens can be virtual barrier for pollinators because unless you've persuaded your neighbours to be pollinator savvy, and please, please try, our gardens can become isolated oases within the landscape.

Most pollinators don't travel far from where they hatch or from their nest, and many solitary bees will only forage a few metres from where they emerge. This means that they need a source of food nearby. Some travel a little further afield and these pollinators need a source of energy rich food to sustain their activity. Imagine if they flew far from their nest and couldn't find any flowers to gather nectar. They would be

Empty border space can be quickly and effectively filled by sowing annual flowering plants from seed. © Debi Holland.

isolated and starving and not able to get back. Our gardens, small or large, are dining stations when they are filled with flowers, but gardens near to each other, or patches of flowers on road verges or roundabouts, create corridors or feeding stops to nourish not just bees but all manner of pollinators and creatures that feed on the flowers.

For the pollinators that can and do fly kilometres on a foraging run, imagine that your garden is an oasis on their journey. It's a fast food stop and the more you can do to make it a five star diner the better it will be for them all. If you want to support and encourage pollinators of all sorts the best thing you can do is to plant insect friendly plants, garden organically and stop using pesticides of all kinds.

If you can encourage others in your neighbourhood to do the same you will extend the pollinator friendly zones in your area and help create bigger and better corridors and 'rich areas' of 'flower' forage that all link together.

The Food Chain

Every creature plays a part in nature's entangled web of life. Many are predators and prey, or use another species to complete their lifecycles. The whole food chain and web of nature is intricately woven together like a three dimensional tapestry of life. It's all interconnected, with each level dependent on the one above and the one below to exist, survive and thrive. The bottom layer is mostly made up of plants. In a garden that means your garden plants too! All the creatures that eat your garden plants rely on those plant species to feed their larvae or themselves. Then they become the next layer as food for predators. Some are predators too playing a vital role of 'pest control' in our gardens and in turn may be food for the birds. It's a fragile web that needs every living organism to thrive.

SAVE THE BEES

The media is full of stories on the demise of bees, mostly honeybees! And while the honeybee is rightly revered, (it is after all the only UK bee that makes honey as we know it) it is also the most understood of our pollinators. The honeybee has a club in every town and an army of beekeepers onside to keep it alive and kicking. If only we could say the same for the rest of nature and especially our pollinators. Like the honeybee they are challenged with climate change. An early spring warm spell that encourages early emerging pollinators but which does not coincide with the plants that they need to survive can wreck a whole generation. Loss of habitat, building projects, creeping towns and cities, changes in agriculture and toxic pesticides have all taken their toll. There is probably now only 1 per cent of our ancient wildflower meadows left in the UK. Between the 1930s and 1984 we have destroyed, dug up and built over 97 per cent of them, and since the '80s the true figure is probably 99 per cent or more (Ref 5).

Wildflower meadows are a rare commodity, but we can recreate our own version in our gardens.
© Debi Holland.

SIMPLE WAYS TO SUPPORT POLLINATORS

Gardens will never replace the lost forage of these ancient meadows, but we can help. Many gardeners are adding wildflower meadows to their gardens and there are plenty of other ways to help, which we will explore later in the book. But here are a few to get you started before we meet some pollinators.

Fall in Love With Weeds

So many of the plants regarded as garden weeds are in fact very important for pollinators. Most are native, which doesn't make them better than our garden plants, but what it does mean is that our native bees probably evolved alongside them and have used and needed them as food plants for millennia. Most gardens and collections

Early spring dandelion flowers provide a lifeline for pollinators such as hoverflies (Ersitalis spp). © Jean Vernon.

of plants are curated by a gardener. In a small garden where space is at a premium you might find tolerating weeds a test, so instead I challenge you to find a way to let just some of them grow. It might be letting the lawn grow a little longer so that the wild plants can flower. Or why not plant a pot of dandelions? I am sure if the flowers were pink or purple we would cherish them. And don't forget that for most 'weeds' there are garden-worthy cultivars that are grown widely in gardens across the UK. So you can choose to grow a cultivated form of thistle like artichokes or cardoon. Or grow a cultivated form of bramble that's really good for pollinators and will produce a crop of blackberrries for you or the wildlife.

Embrace All Garden Wildlife

It's important to understand that everything in nature is intricately connected in a tangled web of life. Changing the way we think about 'problems' and embracing and harnessing the power of nature is a huge step forward as we work with nature and not against it. That means welcoming all wildlife, big and small, into your plot and finding a way to live and let live. Snails, for example, might feast on your seedlings, decimate your hostas and hide in the hedge, but for the song thrush they are an important source of food. Once the contents have been devoured, the empty shells are a vital calcium source for nesting birds, and amazingly there is even a rare little bee, the Snail Nester bee, that lays her eggs inside empty snail shells. I can't think of a better waterproof home for her babies.

Plant for All Seasons

I'm going to repeat this throughout the book. The right plants flowering when the pollinators need forage are vital for their survival. It might be caterpillar plants for butterflies and moths, or even aphid susceptible plants where hoverflies may lay their eggs so that their hatching offspring have a source of food. Flowering plants for nectar and pollen are important, but larval food plants are essential. Many species of pollinators feed on specific plant species and only those plants, so it is important to learn a bit about the needs of specific pollinators and how to attract them. The humble and much hated stinging nettle is a great example. Try growing a clump in a large pot to restrict them from spreading and to support the huge diversity of pollinators that use them as larval plant.

Choose a variety of flower shapes, flower colours and plants that flower all the way through from late winter into very early spring, into late autumn and even through winter.

The critical time for queen bumblebees is between winter and spring. Bombus lucorum agg. on Trachystemon orientalis. © Martin Mulchinock.

Dump the Toxins

If you only do one thing to support the pollinators (and the planet), stop using garden chemicals. Not just insecticides and weedkillers, but fungicides and chemical fertilisers too. Instead, harness the power of nature. Encourage wildlife into the garden to feast on the garden mini-beasts. Plant natural bird food plants and make your garden a haven for wild birds. Restore the natural balance in the garden, so that bug eats bug, insect eating birds catch caterpillars to feed to their chicks, and predatory pollinators keep other garden insects under control. Feed your plants by feeding the soil. Improve the soil with homemade garden compost and worm compost, which in turn will support the natural balance of the soil and all the microbes and mini-beasts that live within.

Go low mow or no mow

Pretty much every garden in the UK has a lawn and many form the heart of the garden. Sometimes gardeners are armed with toxic chemicals and other concoctions to weed out the wildflowers and kill moss, and even to deter the gardener's best friend, the worm. But look at a photo of a 'perfect' lawn and then at a softer wildflower meadow, with paths cut through it for access, and ask yourself, which is the prettier effect? Give me a wildflower lawn any day.

The bright yellow flowers of Bird's Foot Trefoil are rich in valuable nectar. © Jean Vernon.

Let the grass grow a bit longer this season, or experiment with a third or a quarter of the area, leaving the lawn 'weeds' to flower, and see what grows. Common wildflowers that grow in garden lawns include ground ivy and daisies, clover and self heal, and bird's foot trefoil. Clover (red or white) and bird's foot trefoil are what I regard as five-star pollinator plants. Both are in the pea family, both fix nitrogen from the air and essentially feed themselves and both have nectar rich flowers that are a life saver for pollinators, including the bees. Several moth species use these plant species as their larval food plants. Bird's foot trefoil is an excellent pollinator plant. It should be in every garden and every lawn. It's a beautiful plant and it will flower in a lawn even when you cut it down to an inch of its life. A lawn full of bird's foot trefoil and clover will stay green forever and hardly ever dry out.

By cutting different sections of the lawn and leaving the rest to flower you are increasing the forage for the wild pollinators. Imagine if every lawn had a pollinator strip. Why not plant some wildflower plug plants into the turf and improve the diversity of the plants within?

ATTRACTING GARDEN POLLINATORS

Provide Water

If you've got room add a pond to the garden. It's the perfect way to bring wildlife to your plot. Even insects need water to drink, breed and moisten materials for their nests. Rainwater is better than tap water, and just a shallow bowl of water will help, preferably filled with pebbles or marbles to create a safe place to reach the water. Provide a ladder escape from deep water and keep your bowl or pond topped up with clean and fresh water.

Make a shallow bee drinker, filled with rain water. © Jean Vernon.

CHAPTER TWO

Meet the Pollinators

Y ou might think that butterflies and bees are the main garden pollinators, and that's a very good starting point. They are great pollinators and some may be so much better than others. But there are many other pollinator characters that live, breed and feed in and around our gardens that are less obvious. Not only are they an animated, visual dimension to the flowerbeds and borders, but they are interconnected, together creating a fascinating 'coral reef' effect in the garden.

I am not an entomologist, nor is this a text book, but I hope it will whet your appetite to learn more about our garden pollinators and that together we can find ways to make our gardens more attractive and supportive to these fascinating and essential creatures. Pollinators aren't limited to these insect families or orders, but let's explore some of our fascinating and fantastic pollinators and how to attract them into your garden.

Hoverfly (Eristalis perinax) on scabious. © Jean Vernon.

Butterflies

These are the fairyesque angels of the garden. Their ephemeral beauty never fails to entrance those that stop to admire and stare. Butterflies are the perfect way to get children interested in plants and nature for so many reasons, but especially because these beauties are important pollinators.

Butterflies are graceful, beautiful insects, with huge wings that sail across the air with their sweeping movement. You can't fail to notice them as they alight on the garden flowers with their wings outstretched in all their finery. Their wings are virtual solar panels, tracking the sun and harnessing its warmth to help raise their energy and facilitate flight.

But these beauties also have a dark side that is not always popular with gardeners. One or two species, and it is really just that, can become a problem on a few garden plants, namely cabbages and members of the cabbage family. The rest are a fabulous addition to the garden, are vital pollinators and a great way to get everyone hooked into the fascinating world of insects.

Butterflies are the classic ugly duckling story, transforming from plant munching caterpillars into beautiful, ethereal creatures with magical wings. Their life cycle is

Butterflies add an ephemeral dimension to the garden and are important pollinators. Tortoiseshell on Verbena bonariensis. © Martin Mulchinock.

fascinating, but not dissimilar to many of our garden pollinators, namely egg to grub (larva), which then pupates into winged adults: butterflies. These amazing winged beauties season our summer gardens with their colourful dance.

Butterflies forage to feed themselves, rather than to feed offspring. They visit the flowers for nectar and don't actively collect pollen, so they pick up less pollen than other pollinators. But they often fly longer distances between flowers, effecting more efficient cross-pollination (Ref 22). This means that they may be considered to be better pollinators than some doorstep foragers like many of the bees.

Gardeners understand that some caterpillars devour a huge amount of plant material. But most of them don't destroy the plants and should be regarded as part of the natural balance of the garden instead of as a pest. Plants are the bottom layer of the food chain.

Caterpillars generally get a bad reputation for being pests though, and that can be their downfall. We need to change our thinking and understand that every creature, even the caterpillar, has a part to play. The reason that there are often lots of caterpillars on plants is because so many become a meal for other garden wildlife. Working with nature in our gardens is vital for the survival of many species on the edge of extinction. If you left the caterpillars alone, they would become essential food for your garden birds and other beneficial garden creatures that we revere. It's all part of the intricate web of life in the garden and by removing one layer of the delicate food chain you create an imbalance that nature struggles to rise above.

Butterfly Plants

If you think of the flowers in your garden as the most important food for butterflies you'd be wrong. Of course the nectar in our garden flowers is important, but it's the caterpillar food plants that really ensure the survival of the species. Each species of butterfly (and moth) have plants that feed their larval stage. And without these specific plants the caterpillars will starve. Butterflies very cleverly find the host plants to lay their eggs, so that the hatching larvae have food immediately to fuel their life stage. They do this by tasting through their feet. When they land on a plant they can check whether the plant is the right type for their caterpillars to thrive. So if there is a butterfly species that you love, by all means plant a few flowers that the adults feed from but it's far more important to learn about the food plants of their caterpillars and plant these too. The adults seek out the correct plants to lay their eggs on, so if those plants are growing in your garden then you have a much better chance of seeing these species.

But it's the adults that are the pollinators. Butterflies don't eat pollen like many pollinators. But by visiting nectar rich flowers to fuel their activity they can pick up pollen grains and move them from flower to flower.

Great nectar plants for butterflies include knapweeds and other members of the thistle family. The wonderful things about knapweed are that they can be grown from seed. They are perennials and free from prickles. Scabious is another brilliant butterfly and pollinator plant. Marjoram is another garden stalwart that will feed all sorts of garden pollinators with its nectar rich flowers, and of course you can harvest the herb leaves for pizza! Plants in the daisy family are great butterfly plants; grow everything from the earlier flowering anthemis to rudbeckias and Michaelmas daisies.

FRIEND OR FOE – CABBAGE WHITE

These are not really called Cabbage White butterflies, not by the experts anyway. There are two species, the Large White (*Pieris brassicae*) and the Small White (*Pieris rapae*), commonly incorrectly referred to by gardeners as Cabbage Whites. And while I am not a fan of the word pest, the Large White is one of two butterfly species that are considered to be pests by gardeners, farmers and growers. If you have ever tried to grow cabbages and cauliflowers this is the species that eats most of the leaves in mid to late summer.

It's a smelly caterpillar because it uses the mustard oils in the cabbages to deter predators. This in itself is fascinating. It's a self-defence mechanism that the plants first employ to deter predators. But since the butterflies and caterpillars evolved

together they have not only become resistant to the toxins, but they can take compounds from plants in a sort of arms race, chemical defence mechanism. In the case of cabbages it is their smelly mustard oils (mustard gas was the chemical agent used in the First World War so gives you a clue to the nature of this compound), that are used. The caterpillars use these bitter, smelly, mustard toxins as a technique to deter predators; birds won't eat them but wasps collect them for their own larvae to eat.

They also have a bright leery livery that shouts 'Don't eat

Caterpillars of Pieris brassicae are brightly coloured en masse and smell horrible. © Jean Vernon.

me!', and generally that works. They also use the safety in numbers trick and those that survive go on to morph into ephemeral adults to 'plague' the gardens nearby. So already you can see several techniques at work with this one species. A healthy nest of 10 blue tits requires 1,000 caterpillars a day to feed the chicks (Ref 23), so your sacrificial cabbages support the wild birds too.

Before you reach for the chemical sprays, let nature take its course. Those plump caterpillars are natural food for insect eating birds and other predators.

The Small White (*Pieris rapae*) is equally interesting. This time the adult lays single eggs spread around your cabbage or kale patch, so you don't get the *en masse* destruction of your plants. The caterpillars are leaf green in colour and hugely camouflaged. The telltale signs are holes in the leaves and lots of dark green caterpillar poo. Look carefully as these caterpillars line up with the leaf veins and can be difficult to spot (see inset image below).

If you can't live with them, don't reach for the chemical spray, simply pick them off or hose them off with a water jet and allow the garden birds to feed them to their chicks.

Caterpillars of Pieris rapae are usually solitary and well camouflaged. © Jean Vernon.

BLUE BUTTERFLIES

A flash of blue wings in the garden is enough to lift your spirits. Few creatures wear the blue livery with such grace as butterflies. In the UK there are nine species of butterfly that wear these shades of blues, from the bright azure blue of the Adonis to the extremely rare Large Blue. Surprisingly, the Common Blue is not the most common butterfly in the UK anymore; the blue males are commonly seen in grassy areas, but the females are less obvious and better camouflaged, often in shades of softer beige or brown.

The fabulous Adonis Blue butterfly (Polyommatus bellargus). © Liam Olds.

The Large Blue is the largest and rarest species of the UK's nine blue butterflies, but it is also the most fascinating. It was extinct in the UK for some time but has been reintroduced using Swedish butterflies; however, it is still restricted to a handful of special sites.

Special needs

The Large Blue (*Phengaris arion*) (Ref 24) is a true beauty. But it is extremely rare and not a garden species. It went extinct and has been reintroduced to England. Its lifecycle is so extreme and fascinating, that it helps to highlight the incredible complexities of some pollinators' existence. This species has a stand-out row of black spots on its top wing. But unless you visit known sites you are unlikely to see this beauty.

What sets it apart from other butterflies is its extremely fascinating life cycle where it spends most of its life as a caterpillar, underground inside red ants' nests, feeding on their grubs. And to make things even more complex it ideally needs a specific red ant species (*Myrmica sabuleti*) and several specific food plants to support its different larval stages.

The eggs are laid singly into the flower heads of wild thyme growing among ant nests. At first the caterpillars feed on the flower heads of wild thyme, but this needs to be growing in closely cropped turf for its host ants to thrive. When the caterpillar larvae are still young they stop eating the thyme leaves and are found by the ants, which feed on sugary secretions that the larvae produce from a special gland.

The caterpillars hunch up and are carried back to the nest chamber by the ants where they become the worst possible house guests, they pretend to be ant larvae, communicating using ultrasound and eating the ant grubs until the butterfly caterpillars are ready to pupate and emerge as adult Large Blue butterflies. The ants actually protect the butterfly larvae so their nests are a safe place for them to mature. (Ref 25 26 27). The adults emerge in June and the cycle begins again. So it's no wonder that this butterfly is rare. Without the specific species of ant and indeed the correct plants for forage it can't complete its lifecycle.

The very rare Large Blue (Phengaris arion) on pyramidal orchid. © Lance Featherstone.

Holly Blue (*Celastrina argiolus*)

Unlike most of the other blue species of butterflies, the Holly Blue (Ref 28) emerges earlier in spring, flies above the grass level and uses garden plants for its larval food rather than grasses like other blue species. Instead, it lays its eggs on the flower buds, berries and young leaves of holly in spring and a second, later, summer generation feeds on ivy. In my book its penchant for holly and ivy makes it a festive butterfly. Holly Blue is a widespread species with a southern emphasis, but it is spreading northwards, presumably with climate change. Like most species some years are better for this blue beauty than others.

How to spot
If you find a blue butterfly in a park or garden it is most likely to be the Holly Blue, especially in early spring. This is quite a bright blue butterfly. The females have a black edge to their forewings. On the pale blue underside of the wings

are small black spots, unlike the Common Blue, which has brown shaded underside and a mix of black, white and orange/beige spots.

The Holly Blue is a common sight along hedgerows and the edges of woodland, so gardens bordering the countryside are more likely to attract this species.

How to attract

The Holly Blue has two lifecycles a year. And interestingly the first brood will feed on holly, while the later brood prefers ivy. Cater for them both and grow more holly and ivy in your garden. Female holly plants (the ones that bear berries) are better than the males.

Look out for the more common Holly Blue (Celastrina argiolus) in your garden, on persicaria. © Jean Vernon.

Ilex aquifolium 'JC Van Tol' is a self-fertile female plant that can be grown alone without the need for an additional pollinator. It has prickle free leaves too so it is a good choice if you have a young family or inquisitive pets.

Ilex x merserveae 'Blue Princess' is a gorgeous plant with rich blue green leaves, and blood red berries. Holly is relatively slow growing so for instant impact buy a large plant.

Plant holly along the boundaries as part of a native hedge and let the ivy flower. While these are the main larval plants, Holly Blue larvae will also feed on other garden plants such as the colourful stemmed dogwoods (cornus), spindle bushes, but also the more rampant, and wilder brambles, gorse and snowberries (Ref 29). Don't forget to ensure there are nectar rich flowers for the adults of both broods. In spring the bugle and forget-me-not are excellent pollinator plants. Bugle is a wonderful garden ground cover plant. If you have a wildflower patch add red campion and buttercups. Later flowers like thistles, mint, privet and brambles provide nectar for this species.

Painted Lady (*Vanessa cardui*)

This is a creature that deserves our complete admiration; in fact the story of its remarkable life is the stuff of science fiction and fairytale. The Painted Lady is not a resident UK species but a migrant, often arriving to UK shores in large numbers each summer. Like many creatures it arrives in Britain to feed. Scientists believe that it sets off from its native lands in north Africa when the density of the population there threatens the availability of food. (Ref 30).

Up until recently (2009) (Ref 31) it was believed that Britain was a dead end for this incredible migratory insect, which is unable to survive the British winter when its food plants aren't growing, and while commonly recorded in British summers it was never seen leaving. Our native butterflies hibernate as adults or pupae whereas most migrants fly south to warmer lands. Special entomological radars were used to track these butterflies flying southwards in later summer at a height of 500 metres where the prevailing wind enabled them to fly south at 30mph. Scientists discovered that the Painted Lady is controlled by day length. Caterpillars developing while the days are getting longer become adults that fly northwards. As the days shorten the emerging butterflies are aware of the need to travel south.

So one individual butterfly doesn't fly the full 5,000 miles to the UK, and instead the journey is completed over several generations as a progressional journey. Most start as caterpillars in Africa and as spring begins they move north over the Sahara desert, some getting as far as southern Europe, while others reach north Africa. The next generation continues northwards to the UK. But some have been found to fly the 5,000 miles back. Please record any sightings at Butterfly Conservation (Ref 32).

How to spot

The Painted Lady butterfly is a large orange butterfly with black tips to its forewings and white and black spots. You can find it between April and October, though it is more common in mid to late summer. It often feeds on buddleia flowers. It cannot survive our winters.

How to attract

Grow plenty of nectar rich summer flowers to provide a nectar bar for garden butterflies. Painted Lady caterpillars feed on thistles, nettles, mallows and viper's bugloss. By providing these larval host plants you could get a generation of these migrants breeding in your garden.

The incredible Painted Lady (Vanessa cardui) has a fascinating story to tell. © Jean Vernon.

Peacock (*Aglais io*)

The Peacock butterfly is a much-loved British butterfly species. It is commonly seen in our gardens, has beautiful patterns on its wings and it often overwinters as an adult so you might find them hibernating in your house or garden shed.

Just like the peacock bird, the Peacock butterfly has large eyespots on its wings, which are an important feature of this species (Ref 33). It uses these spots in two different ways.

Its underwings are black and because it overwinters as an adult butterfly it can hide in almost any shadow because it is black on the inside. When disturbed it makes quite a loud rustling sound with its wings. To a would-be predator that might be enough to put it off as it sounds like a larger creature. But if the sound doesn't work then it will flash its wings open revealing its large 'eyes'.

This gives it the appearance of a predator, or an owl or an aggressive mammal and acts as a frightener to a potential predator. Even if this tactic only gives it a few seconds head start it can be enough to allow it to escape. Plus, the eyes become a target for a predator and if only the wing is damaged then the butterfly can still go on to breed.

The stunning Peacock butterfly (Aglais io) has dramatic 'eyes' on its wings. © Jean Vernon.

The Peacock butterfly tends to have one brood a year. They overwinter as adults and mate and lay their eggs in spring. The pupae emerge as adults in late summer, feed a bit and then go into hibernation.

How to spot

The Peacock is an easy butterfly to identify thanks to its large eyes and colourful livery. Use a good butterfly ID book or website. The caterpillars are black with a spangly white spotted effect and are found feeding on stinging nettles, usually *en masse*.

Keep a watch for butterfly larvae. These Peacock butterfly caterpillars need nettles to complete their life cycle. © Jean Vernon.

How to attract

Leave a few nettles to grow and mature in a sunny spot, more if you can. You are unlikely to be able to grow enough nettles for the ravenous masses of the Peacock's larvae, but other species will benefit. Grow more nectar plants like knapweed, scabious, marjoram, and daises like anthemis, rudbeckia, and Michaelmas daisies.

Avoid all pesticides and buy organic plants where possible.

Brimstone (*Gonepteryx rhamni*)

The buttery yellow wings of this beautiful butterfly are thought to be how butterflies got their name: butter coloured fly. The Brimstone butterfly has one of the longest lifespans of any UK butterfly (9–10 months) and overwinters as an adult. This is quite unusual in butterflies and means that you may see its buttery yellow, leaf shaped wings flitting around the garden or in woodlands on warmer winter days. It also means you might see it at any time of the year. It is most commonly seen in our gardens in April and May when the adults emerge from hibernation. They will feed on dandelion flowers, primroses, cowslips, bugle and bluebells. In August, when the new adults emerge, the new butterflies need plenty of nectar to sustain them through the long winter, so look out for them on purple/blue flowers such as buddleia, thistles and Devil's-bit-scabious.

The Brimstone butterfly has a southern biased distribution but can be found as far north as Cheshire and south-east Yorkshire (Ref 34). Eggs are usually laid on alder buckthorn and buckthorn, which are not typical garden plants and are much more likely to be found in hedgerows, riverbanks and scrubland. If you have one of these plants in or near your garden you can virtually guarantee that the Brimstone butterfly will find it. These plants are easy to include in a boundary hedge and aren't especially prickly.

The buttery yellow Brimstone butterfly (Gonepteryx rhamni) is a spring and summer beauty. © Martin Mulchinock.

How to spot

There are a few yellow species of butterfly that you might see in your garden, but the Brimstone is fairly easy to identify. It looks a bit like a leaf. It's the male that is the rich yellow colour; the female is much paler and can be mistaken for a Large White. The green caterpillars have a distinctive movement where they lift off a leaf with an almost hump backed posture.

How to attract

You might not have room to grow buckthorn in your garden, but it could be grown as part of a native hedge. If you garden near woodland then the larval plants of the Brimstone may well be present. But you can grow shrubs and perennials with nectar rich flowers for the adults to feed, such as buddleias, scabious and ornamental thistles.

Buckthorn isn't that easy to identify. It looks a bit like blackthorn (sloe) but the flowers are yellowy brown (not white) and the berries are smaller. It's more likely to be in woody scrubland. It's not as spiny as blackthorn and can be planted in a hedge, but beware of pruning it when the caterpillars are present from April to late June.

CLIMATE CHANGE

Butterflies use the sun to kick-start their activity but they aren't very good at controlling their body temperature (Ref 35). Instead, some of them, like the Brown Argus and the Small Copper choose a micro-habitat at the correct temperature to help regulate their temperature, but have suffered larger population declines. Recent research from the University of Cambridge has shown that larger and paler butterflies such as the Large White and Brimstone are better able to buffer themselves against temperature changes by angling their wings to the sun and deflecting the heat from or to their bodies depending on their needs. These appear to have more stable populations.

The populations of two-thirds of UK butterfly species are in decline: habitat loss and fragmentation, and more monotonous landscapes,

The Brown Argus (Aricia agestis) is much less common now. On marjoram flowers. © Lance Featherstone.

have removed many of the micro-climates butterflies need to survive. Climate change is compounding the problem by causing more extreme weather events and greater fluctuations in temperature.

By providing shady spots in the garden, gardeners can help to protect butterflies from climate change. Patches of grass can be allowed to grow longer to create cooler, shady places for butterfly species. In larger landscapes and even large gardens, features such as hedges, woodland planting and even ditches that offer a diversity of heights create a wider range of temperatures and more micro-climates to suit different butterfly species.

BUTTERFLY SECRETS

Butterflies can pick up chemical smells using their antennae, but the main receptors are on their feet. When a female butterfly is ready to lay her eggs she lands on a plant that looks right. She doesn't always get it right the first time, but the first thing that she does is to scrape at it with her feet. She can tell a lot about the plant from that. First, is it the right species to feed her offspring? Then is it healthy or dying or suffering from drought or some other problem? She needs to decide whether it is worth laying her eggs there.

Hedge Garlic – Important Butterfly Plant

There are two species of butterfly that need the hedge garlic to complete their life cycle: the Orange Tip and the Green-veined White. Neither of these will damage your vegetables and both are a beautiful, exotic addition to your garden. The Green-veined White likes nasturtiums and other weeds like shepherd's purse, but lays single eggs so you don't get masses of caterpillars devouring your plants. The Orange Tip specialises in seedpods and lays its eggs on the garlic mustard when it flowers. Garlic mustard or

Remember that different butterflies need specific plants for survival. The Orange Tip (Anthocharis cardamines) on herb Robert (Geranium robertianum). © Martin Mulchinock.

hedge garlic is a great spring plant to add a bit of spice to salads. Let it grow and you are providing food for two species of butterfly.

A Group of Butterflies is Called a Flutter.

Most adult butterflies don't usually live very long: 3–4 weeks is the average lifespan. But some, like the Peacock and the Brimstone, spend a lot longer as adults and overwinter as adults.

Camouflage

Butterflies often have a drab underwing. They roost with their wings closed so that the drab underside helps camouflage them from predators.

Solar Powered

Butterflies only fly in the daytime. They are solar powered and fuelled with nectar

The dark underside of butterflies is effective camouflage. Peacock butterfly (Aglais io) on Buddleia x weyeriana. © Martin Mulchinock.

so they need sunshine and flowers to fly. When they first wake in the morning butterflies will sit with their wings open or partly open absorbing the heat of the sun. This activates them and then they will start to feed on the flowers. The flowers provide them with energy-rich nectar that enables them to fly.

Butterflies have hairy and usually dark bodies that heat up faster in the sun and hold the heat for longer. Even when the ambient temperature in the UK is around 15°C the butterfly's body temperature will be about 35°C from sunbathing and by using their flight muscles.

When the sun goes down the butterflies will find a place to roost and shut their wings so that they remain camouflaged.

Scale Effect

Butterflies have scales. All that colour on their wings is created by thousands of light-reflecting scales. They find their mates visually by the colour of their wings rather than by chemical scent.

Damage Limitation

The Speckled Wood is so successful because it has numerous broods throughout the year and because it can spend the winter either as a chrysalis or as a caterpillar. Its caterpillars feed on grass so there are plenty of food plants and when the weather is poor it has fewer broods.

The Speckled Wood butterfly (Pararge aegeria) has adapted so that it can breed throughout the year. © Martin Mulchinock.

STINGING NETTLES

You might have uncomfortable memories of stinging nettles from childhood, but here's your chance to fall in love with them again. First, nettles are native plants to the UK, which means that they have evolved to live here and partly explains why they are such a successful plant. But did you know that nettles are edible? If you steam the young leaves (pick with care), they taste a bit like spinach and can be used in a variety of ways in your menus. So a decent patch of nettles is a fantastic source of vitamin rich leaves for pesto, quiche, bakes, stir fries and much, much more. If society collapsed tomorrow we would depend on nettles. Try drying the flowers and add them to salt. You can even make wine or beer from the leaves. Add the leaves to the compost heap and they act as an accelerator: as they break down their leaves release nutrients to the composting microbes. Or use the stems to make string or cloth.

But don't be too hasty harvesting the leaves because there are several butterfly and moth species that rely on these plants as larval food. Not only are they a good, organic source of fibre and nutrients for us, but also for five of the most colourful garden butterflies: Peacock, Small Tortoiseshell, Comma, Red Admiral and the Painted Lady. It is also a food plant for some moths.

The caterpillars of these species feed on the leaves of nettles. If you have a patch of nettles in a sunny place, keep a watch for signs of butterfly eggs and maturing caterpillars. Check carefully and if your nettles are not feeding butterfly larvae and are clear of butterfly eggs then cut half the clump down to about six inches above the ground. This is a gardening technique affectionately called the Chelsea Chop as it's done around the time of the annual Chelsea flower show in mid to late May. The idea is that you encourage the plants to make fresh shoots, leaves and indeed

Stinging nettles are fantastic plants for pollinators and incredibly useful for gardeners. © Martin Mulchinock.

flowers, and that staggers the plants' development. For gardeners and of course for pollinators, spreading the flowering time of established clumps of flowers is of huge benefit. But when it comes to nettles it's the new leaves we want, so that the butterflies have plenty of fresh growth to lay their eggs and feed their offspring.

You can grow nettles in pots and if you place them deep into the flower border you are less likely to be stung by the leaves and you will help confine them to the pot and not spread via underground stems. If you have two large pots you can cut one down in late May and the other down in July to keep them producing leaves. Put the chopped up stems onto the compost heap to make compost to feed the soil and you have helped to complete the natural cycle of life, death and regrowth.

Other Good Butterfly Plants

Hops are a magnet for the Comma butterfly and it's a useful plant for hiding eyesores. It's not an evergreen, but it's a fast grower and will grow and clamber to cascade over an ugly outbuilding or garden post.

Grasses are great for butterflies, but not as closely cropped lawns. Let the lawn grow and cut it once a year in autumn. Leave the cut grass to dry and drop its seeds for a few days and then compost it. Plant plug plants of wildflowers into the area or sow wildflower seeds to create a patch that is far more full of life than a mown lawn. Most of the brown butterflies, like the Speckled Wood, the Small Heath, the Gatekeeper, the Meadow Brown and the Large and Small Skippers all feed on grass species as caterpillars and they aren't that fussy as to which species, so by not cutting the grass, you are adding a whole new level of larval food plants to your garden.

Many species of grass are important larval plants for butterflies and moths. © *Martin Mulchinock.*

ATTRACTING GARDEN POLLINATORS

Moths

My earliest memories of garden moths go back to my childhood garden. We had two very mature and very dark flowered lilac trees in the garden where I grew up. They had split trunks and were perfect for climbing. The bark was so tactile and I loved peeling strips from the trunk. But it was the deep purple fragrant flowers that really gave the wow factor. All the other lilacs around were the soft pale, lilac colour and I loved the fact that ours were dark and different. It was beneath one of the lilacs that I found my first moth. What a beauty. It was white and fluffy with black markings, but looked like a fluffy mouse with angel wings. I suspect it was a White Ermine moth and I don't think I have seen one since. As a six-year-old I was mesmerised. Its beauty and fragility were awesome and I don't think I really believed it wasn't an angel or a garden fairy. It is etched in my memory and a poignant reminder of the importance of showing children the wonders of nature. You just never know what flame will ignite from a spark of interest.

I often think it's strange that moths appear to be the poor cousins of the butterflies. Perhaps its because many are night-flying and we don't see them as often as we might spot butterflies in and around the garden? Or is it because many of the moth's larval stages are regarded as garden pests that we have mistakenly relegated the moths to a lower division of our respect?

If we are to really make a difference to the natural world we need to remove these boundaries that we silently set on nature. We cannot pick and choose the creatures we want to support; each and every one has a place in our gardens and even in excess they provide a rich source of food for something else.

The fantastical Pale Tussock moth (Calliteara pudibunda) is just one of the secret moth pollinators in your garden. © Gail Ashton.

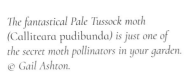

Moths Matter

In the UK moths are numerous and widespread (Ref 36), but they are still underappreciated and often overlooked. With approximately 2,500 different species within the United Kingdom living in a wide range of habitats including our gardens, the diversity of moths is astounding. But the abundance of the larger moths in the UK has crashed over the last 40 years or so and three species have become extinct this century. Moths don't have the cute factor of the mega fauna like elephants and tigers, and maybe it is their smaller, more inconspicuous presence that makes them seem dispensable. But moths are vital pollinators, often working with the night-scented plants that open at night, and have their own needs in terms of larval food plants. Moth caterpillars may be considered to be a menace by some gardeners but they are actually a vital food source for a wide range of our garden wildlife. Most of our favourite garden birds rely on moth caterpillars to feed their chicks. Blue Tit chicks eat an estimated 35 billion moth caterpillars a year (Ref 37). If garden owners are spray happy, administering toxic chemicals to their plants, then they are wiping out a whole section of the food chain. Blue tits, great tits, robins, wrens and blackbirds devour vast quantities of this natural food. Bats, frogs, toads, lizards, slowworms, snakes and small mammals also feed on moths and their larvae.

CHEMICAL WARFARE

Many butterflies and moths utilise pheromone smells, toxic chemicals and even viruses to outwit host plants, find a mate and fend off attack by predators and parasites (Ref 38). Some of these evolutionary traits are hard to believe.

Moths evolved before butterflies some 100 millions of years ago. The earliest moths were called Psychidae and probably evolved from a species like a Caddisfly. They are thought to have crawled from bogs and feasted on primitive non flowering plants like lichen and mosses.

The early moth species then co-evolved with the primitive flowering plants, and the day-flying nectar dependent species we now call butterflies would have developed around 100 to 160 million years ago. So in geological time butterflies are a very recent addition.

The species evolved together to form a myriad of interconnected and mutualistic relationships, basically because the flowers need the insects and the insects need the flowers.

In effect butterflies are moths that fly in the daytime, but the best way to tell the two apart is the antennae. Butterflies have a hair like antennae with a club at the tip, whereas moths rarely have that.

ATTRACTING GARDEN POLLINATORS

Most moths don't have the club or instead may have feathery antennae that are used to 'smell' pheromones, particularly to find a mate. The feathery structure has a greater surface area to detect the scent of a female and the females use their antenna to find their larval food plants to lay their eggs. Many moths fly at night, so they don't use visual cues to find a mate and are often more drab in colour and better camouflaged. The day flying moths are usually brighter and more colourful and rely on visual characteristics to locate their mate.

Some moths have quite incredible ways of taking toxins from the plants that they feed on as caterpillars to give them a defense as adults, making them toxic or inedible as caterpillars or as the adult moth. One extreme example of this is the rare migrant moth, the Spurge Hawk moth, which has specialised in feeding on one of the most toxic groups of plants, the euphorbias or spurges. The Spurge Hawk moth caterpillar can't stomach the sap, instead it chews through the stem of the plant so that it wilts and the sap is lost, and then the moth eats the wilted parts of the plant. The adult moth is a precious pollinator.

Greedy Babes

One of the most fascinating things about moths is that not all moths are pollinators. Just because an insect visits a flower doesn't make it a pollinator. But moths are an enigma. There are a lot of moths, for example the saturniid large family of moths, that don't feed at all as adults. They store sufficient food as caterpillars to take them through the year, which makes the caterpillar stage even more important. There is just one saturniid moth known in the UK, the stunning Emperor moth.

Moths that don't feed as adults at all are thought to have evolved before the flowers, so they didn't have an opportunity to feed as adults and so never needed to. But primitive moths that evolved before flowers are thought to have fed on tree sap or possibly sweet honeydew exuded by other insects.

Some of the moth caterpillars are quite extraordinary. Vapourer moth (Orgyia antiqua) is a common garden visitor. © Jean Vernon.

Instead these species feed voraciously as caterpillars and store enough food as caterpillars to take them through the resting pupal stage, emergence, mating and laying eggs, so they have enough energy to take them through their whole lifecycle.

The Vapourer moth is very common in gardens, is brightly coloured and completely harmless – and doesn't feed as an adult. The female is sedentary, virtually just a bag of eggs, and can't even fly.

Moths that do feed, visit flowers for nectar and pick up pollen as they move around the flowers. Previous research into the transport of pollen by moths focused on their proboscis, but their feathery bodies collect pollen as they settle on flowers and move it onto the flower's stigmas as they move around.

Moths to a Flame

Why are moths attracted to the light? What we know so far is that moths can fly roughly in a straight line by keeping a set angle to natural light, so in effect they use stars or the moon as a guide. So when we produce artificial light that is too close, and then they keep a fixed angle to that artificial light, they finish up spiralling. We're actually messing up their navigation system (Ref 38).

Butterfly Conservation (Ref 40) is working to save butterflies, moths and their habitats. Why not become a member?

Moth Larval Plants

Nettles are great plants for many butterflies but they are good plants for several moths too. The Mother of Pearl moth, which is a large micro-moth that flies day and night, is a buff straw colour but in the light its wings have a mother of pearl iridescence. There is also a very gorgeous moth called the Burnished Brass moth that looks like it has metallic blotches on its wings and also specialises on nettles as a host plant for its eggs and larvae.

One of the best things you can do in your garden for butterflies and moths is to let the lawn grow. Many species depend on different grasses to lay their eggs and for larval food. If you've got a lawn just stop cutting it and see what happens, or leave part of it to grow long and flower. You can even mow shorter paths through the longer grass. Chances are you've already got a variety of great pollinator plants growing and it will allow the grasses to mature, many of which are important larval plants for a wide variety of species. Cut it in early autumn, leave the clippings for a few days to drop their seeds and then rake them up and compost them. Add some wildflower plugs and let them establish over the winter. Then repeat.

The pretty flowers of bird's foot trefoil are perfect for a pollinator lawn. © Jean Vernon.

Butterfly Conservation has a few downloadable leaflets on garden moths and larval food plants (Ref 39).

DAY-FLYING MOTHS

Moths are sometimes described as night-flying butterflies, but that does not fit a large proportion of moth species, because many moth species only fly in the daylight. Some moths fly day and night, and there are also many species that are much more active during the day. Usually, but of course there are exceptions, the day-flying moths are more colourful than their night flying relations, possibly because they use visual characteristics to not just find their partner but also to deter predators.

Silver Y Moth (*Autographa gamma*)

Silver Y moth (Ref 41) is a common moth in our gardens; it flies by day and by night. It's not British, it's one of our commonest immigrants and migrates here every year. It eats all sorts of things as a caterpillar and it's occasionally a pest in greenhouses on tomatoes. It's a very rapid flyer and can be confused with the Humming-bird Hawk moth because that behaves in the same way.

Look out for the metallic 'Y' autograph on the Silver Y moth (Autographa gamma). © Martin Mulchinock.

Originally from southern Europe and Africa the Silver Y Moth migrates and breeds here every year in vast quantities. Research from the University of Exeter (Ref 42) discovered using radar just quite how extraordinary this moth's migrational powers are. Researchers (Ref 43) discovered that the Silver Ys were flying at altitudes that made the best use of tailwinds. The radar showed that the moths were even able to orientate their bodies to compensate for crosswinds. It also revealed that these tiny moths were travelling as fast, if not faster than migrating birds.

How to spot
This is a common species in our gardens and is pretty easy to identify by its markings. On each forewing there is a metallic silvery Y, hence its name. Otherwise it is a mottled beige, grey and brown medium moth that is more common in late summer and into autumn. It's a fast flying species and is often seen feeding on garden flowers just before dusk.

How to attract
The Silver Y moth is commonly found in gardens, but will also be present in a variety of other habitats. Its caterpillars feed on a variety of plants including nettles, clovers, garden peas and cabbages, so by growing these crops and allowing the nettles and clovers to establish somewhere on your plot you are providing essential larval food plants for this species and many others.

ATTRACTING GARDEN POLLINATORS

Mint Moth (*Pyrausta aurata*)

This pretty little moth flies day and night and is common in gardens, where you might find adults resting on the leaves of mint plants or closely related species (Ref 44). It has a tapestry like appearance with dusky red forewings, splashed with ginger and conspicuous spots of golden yellow. This is a pollinator species; the adults feed and meet atop some common garden plants, transferring pollen from flower to flower. The adult females lay their eggs on a variety of common garden plants in the mint family, such as mint species, catmints, marjoram, sage and thymes. Most of these are culinary herbs that you are probably growing somewhere in your garden. Although we tend to use the leaves of these herbs in our herbal teas and menus, herbs also flower and these flowers produce nectar and pollen that have been shown to contain powerful medicinal effects. Some research has shown that bumblebees appear to feed from medicinal herbs when in need of their therapeutic effects (Ref 45).

How to spot
If you find a small dusky red moth on your garden mint or relatives the chances are you've found the mint moth. Look out for its golden yellow spots on the forewings and it's rich tapestry-like look. The caterpillars are black and green with a brown head.

How to attract
Plant a herb garden and fill it with generous clumps of plants in the mint family. Use the fresh tips for herbal tea and ingredients in your summer menus, but allow

The Mint moth (Pyrausta aurata) is a common garden visitor. © Jean Vernon.

the plants to flower and set seed too. Keep the plants flowering for longer by using the Chelsea Chop technique, cutting back a third of the plant shoots by two thirds in mid to late May. You can use this technique on most herbaceous perennials to extend their flowering season, but do keep a look out for caterpillars feeding on the foliage and avoid cutting those to ensure these moths have plenty of larval food.

Humming-Bird Hawk Moth (*Macroglossum stellatarum*)

If you've ever spotted the Humming-bird Hawk moth in your garden the chances are at first sight that you thought it was a humming bird. It's small, flies very fast and hovers at a slight distance from your garden flowers, supping nectar from their nectaries. It's a very beautiful creature and flits from flower to flower in the summer garden feeding on verbena, lavender, buddleia and other nectar rich flowers. Nectar plants are abundant in our gardens, but it's the larval food plants that are less likely to be present. If your garden borders meadows and countryside then the caterpillar plants may be growing nearby. That helps the Humming-bird Hawk moth because most of its favourite larval food plants are not really garden plants. It needs bedstraws, but unless you grow it in a meadow area, or maybe in a pot or a rockery, it doesn't really grow well in most gardens.

Lavender is the perfect nectar flower for long-tongued moths like the Humming-bird Hawk moth (Macroglossum stellatarum). © Martin Mulchinock.

The Humming-bird Hawk moth is another migratory immigrant; it is likely that it does spend the winter in Britain some years, probably as a chrysalis. There is a similar looking Convolvulus Hawk moth which is another migrant that can be found in our summer gardens. Like its name suggests this one feeds as a caterpillar on *Convolvulus spp* including the two forms of bind weed that are the bane of gardeners' lives. You might see the adults feeding on summer flowering tobacco plants.

How to spot
Look out for the Humming-bird Hawk moth in your summer gardens. It has a soft peachy pink body and a long proboscis. You will probably see it on a hot sunny day when out in your garden. It flies very fast and hovers above and in front of flowers that it feeds from, poking its long tongue into the tubular flowers to reach the rich and sugary nectar inside.

How to attract
If you really want to see this amazing species in your garden take a look at any nearby countryside and try and find bedstraws growing nearby. See if you can add them into your garden. Buy some plug plants and add to a flower rich grass planting or meadow. Another plant that the adults might lay their eggs on is red valerian and the adults might also take nectar from its flowers.

If you do see this moth in your garden try and take some photos, though it is notoriously difficult to get a good shot because they fly so fast. Make a note of the flowers that they are feeding from and report your sighting to Migrant Watch with Butterfly Conservation (Ref 46).

CINNABAR MOTH (*TYRIA JACOBAEAE*)

While Cinnabar moths aren't regarded as pollinators they do congregate on flower heads waiting for a mate and will undoubtedly move pollen around by this behaviour. The females don't usually fly until they have mated, but they and many other insects rely on the nectar and pollen rich, yellow ragwort flowers.

This moth is a bit of a conundrum because it relies on one larval plant that is regarded as a huge problem in the countryside – ragwort.

The Cinnabar moth (Tyria jacobaeae) keeps ragwort controlled and needs it to survive. © Gail Ashton.

But it is this moth's dependence on just one plant that makes it fascinating. It feeds as a caterpillar on the toxic flowers and foliage of the ragwort plant. The toxins, types of heart stopping alkaloids, are taken into the body of the caterpillar making them poisonous to eat. They make no secret of this as they sport one of the most dramatic warning dresses of their kind, bright orange and deep black stripes, screaming danger and stop. And the toxins are also present in the equally dramatic looking adult moths. Its blood red underwings and red spotted and striped, black forewings have

Look out for the amber and black stripy caterpillars of the a distinct Dracula appearance *Cinnabar moth. © Jean Vernon.* and again ward off predators.

What is fascinating about this moth–plant relationship is that it creates a balance. The Cinnabar moth is actually the perfect natural control for this perceived nuisance plant.

Burnet Moths (*Zygaena filipendulae/ Zygaena trifolii*)

Another great bunch of pollinators are the Burnet moths; they are a common sight in rural areas and indeed our gardens. They fly mostly in daylight and feed on flowers.

Like the similarly coloured Cinnabar moth the Burnets are toxic to their predators. The caterpillars of the Burnet moths can metabolise toxins from their food plants for their own use. Cyanide is a naturally occurring poison, present in tiny quantities in apple pips, but the Burnet moths can actually make hydrogen cyanide themselves. It is extremely poisonous and it is thought that one Burnet moth is so packed with cyanide it could kill two men. And yet it isn't designed to do that or even to kill its predators. When under attack the Burnet moths release a yellow liquid that is full of alkaloids, including hydrogen cyanide. It tastes disgusting and any predator that comes close to eating one will quickly stop and be put off for life, thus saving the

ATTRACTING GARDEN POLLINATORS

moth and its subsequent offspring. It is also thought that the females release plumes of the chemical to attract a mate (Ref 47, Ref 48).

The caterpillars aren't quite as conspicuous as the Cinnabar moth larvae but they are yellow and black, another warning to predators to avoid. Adults feed on the nectar from scabious, knapweeds and thistles. The caterpillars rely on bird's foot trefoil as a larval food plant.

How to spot

Look out for black winged moths flying in daylight with five or six red spots on each forewing. There are a few closely related species. You might see them nectaring on suitable garden plants, in wildlife meadow plantings and in neighbouring countryside.

Red clover (Trifolium pratense) is an important nectar source for pollinators like the Burnet moths (Zygaena spp). © Martin Mulchinock.

How to attract

Plant bird's foot trefoil. You can grow it in hanging baskets, plant it in pots, add it to a rockery or plant plug plants into a lawn or wildflower meadow. This one plant is one of the very best plants to grow for moths. It's also a good bee plant and provides nectar for a wide range of pollinators.

Add some thistle plants to your borders. There are lots of ornamental varieties such as the globe thistles, which are great pollinator plants. Globe artichokes are an edible and very pollen/nectar rich choice, or the plume thistle is a prickle free choice with gorgeous claret red flowers. Or plant knapweed. It's a top quality nectar plant for pollinators with all the positives of thistles without the spikes.

NIGHT-FLYING MOTHS

Unless you disturb them in the garden, most moths are night-flying. While you may not see these in your night garden unless you go out looking for them or set up a moth trap, you may still get a glimpse of them from time to time and it's important to understand that they are another layer to nature's biodiversity. In fact research by scientists at Newcastle University (Ref 49) found that nocturnal moths contribute a key pollination service for many wild plant families and that some plant species depend on moths for moving pollen. Researchers discovered that the moths carried pollen from 47 insect-pollinated plant species, including from the rose family, bean family, mint family and the umbellifers. Two common plants feature prominently for importance to pollinators and this research highlighted them too. Brambles also known as blackberry and closely related to raspberries and dewberries were shown to be important for nocturnal pollinators along with clovers.

Some of our common garden flowers and indeed our wildflowers are pollinated at night by moths. Night scented plants such as honeysuckle and the white campion emit their seductive scents to attract night flying moths to sample their special brew, tempting them to feed from the flowers in an effort to ensure that they carry pollen from flower to flower. Pale flowers that shine in the moonlight like sweet rocket, phlox and jasmines, long tubular flowers such as honeysuckle and even cup shaped buttercups and evening primroses are all moth-pollinated plants.

Scented flowers that glow in the moonlight like sweet rocket (Hesperis matronalis) are often pollinated by night flying moths. © Jean Vernon.

Buff-Tip Moth (*Phalera bucephala*)

The Buff-tip moth is a great lesson in camouflage; the adult moths look just like a twig, especially side on. It's a combination of the bark-like mottled effect of its wings and the way it positions itself. It looks exactly like a twig and is easily camouflaged among tree stems and branches. It's a common moth that flies at night, usually after midnight, but you might find them resting on a twig during the daytime.

Commonly seen in light traps, it's a beauty. Its caterpillars are hairy and yellow and black, commonly feeding on a range of garden and hedgerow trees, like willow, birch, oak and hazel, but also alder, lime, beech, rowan, hornbeam and sycamore (Ref 50).

How to spot
If you take part in a night-time moth event, or can place a light trap out in the summer garden you may well find this moth. Or if you are lucky you could spot it resting in or under hedges, trees and woodland areas.

Right: *The Buff-tip moth (*Phalera bucephala*) uses twig like camouflage to stay safe in the daylight.* © Martin Mulchinock.

Below: *Buff-tip caterpillars feed on willow leaves.* © Jean Vernon.

How to attract

Choose to plant and grow a rich diversity of trees in your garden. Allow caterpillars to feed; they are unlikely to kill your plants and will metamorphose into adults in due course, or become vital food for birds and insect predators. Live and let live and allow your garden biodiversity to reach its own natural balance.

The Garden Tiger Moth (*Arctia caja*)

The Garden Tiger is quite a striking moth that mostly flies at night, but uses its vivid livery to deter birds and other predators during daylight (Ref 51).

Its main predators are bats, which seek out night flying insects for their diet using ultrasound. This moth has ears on its thorax, not on its head, and can hear bats. Bats can't see the moth's bright livery and so don't know the moth is not good to eat. If the moth detects a bat, it folds its wings and drop like a stone. If it makes it to the tops of a tree, bush or the grass before the bat gets to it, it will survive. But what it also does when it hears the bat is it sends a sonar warning to the bat, telling it that it is a toxic meal. If the bat has never encountered this moth before it might have a go at catching it but will quickly be put off by the taste and hopefully drops the moth. But it will also remember if it hears that sound again that this moth is not worth eating.

Garden Tiger moths generally don't feed as adults so may not be great pollinators but they have two relatives that feed on flowers and in more recent years are becoming more common in gardens, they are the beautiful Scarlet and Jersey Tigers.

*The Garden Tiger moth (*Arctia caja*) flies at night. © Lance Featherstone.*

How to spot

You can't miss the vibrant livery of the Garden Tiger moth. Its forewings are black and cream in an almost leopard skin effect, and its underwings are orange red with black spots. Its caterpillar, affectionately known as the Woolly Bear, is a dark brown fluffy creature with lighter brown stripe along the top. Look out for it crossing paths in summer.

How to attract

The Garden Tiger moth lays its eggs on a wide range of garden plants and also nettles, docks and burdocks, and these are its larval food plants. If you can allow a few of these to grow on your plot you will support a wide range of different species.

Privet Hawk Moth (*Sphinx ligustri*)

This spectacular moth is the UK's largest resident Hawk moth (Ref 52).

Despite its amazing colouration this moth flies mostly at night, attracted by light and sweet night-scented flowers. In the UK in the 1930s and '40s privet hedges were common in suburban gardens and the privet feeding Privet Hawk moth caterpillars thrived. The creamy white flowers are bee magnets, but it is the fresh growth of the plant that is essential for this moth species to thrive. Gardeners encouraged to have neatly pruned privet hedges not only sacrificed the flowers and berries, but also inadvertently pruned out the eggs and caterpillars, breaking the lifecycle of this remarkable moth. Excessive pruning with modern electric and battery powered hedge cutters and the loss of many privet hedges has resulted in a population crash of this species.

The privet hawks lay their eggs on the growth tips and the caterpillars feed on the tips, so when you cut your hedge it's gone, and it is virtually extinct now in most parts of the country. By cutting privet at least twice a year, a common practice,

Hold back pruning your privet plants to give this rare moth a chance to breed. © Brigit Strawbridge-Howard.

gardeners give this species almost no chance whatsoever of surviving. The closely related Swallowtail moth also feeds on privet but it tends to hide in the centre of the bush and feeds at night, so it doesn't get cut off and removed.

How to spot
These iconic moths may be seen resting on tree trunks and fence posts. The bright green caterpillars are magnificent with a curled black tail and vibrant white and purple diagonal stripes.

How to attract
Grow privet and hold back on pruning. Either cut your privet on one side each year, alternating to allow it to mature and the caterpillars to feed, or cut just once a year in autumn when the caterpillars have finished feeding. You will then get the flowers and provide nectar and larval plant food for this species. Privet Hawk moth caterpillars also feed on lilac leaves.

Mullein Moth (*Cucullia verbasci*)

It's not so much the Mullein moth that you might see in your garden, but its rather dramatic caterpillars. The Mullein moth caterpillar is quite spectacular. It feasts on garden verbascum, voraciously munching the leaves, flowers and stems until its ballooning segments are bulging with the brightest yellow bands and black spots. I have them every year on my beautiful perennial verbascum and they have

quite a party feeding on the plants. But they actually sort of do the Chelsea Chop for you, cutting out the growing point of the plant and feasting on the leaves. The plants soon recover, growing back even more strongly and flowering their socks off for the rest of the season. For me the sight of the caterpillars is as exciting as the flowers themselves. The adult moths are camouflaged and brown and twig like. This is another night-flier so unless you put out a moth trap to see which moths are in your garden you are unlikely to notice it.

Live and let live. This spectacular Mullein moth caterpillar will eat your verbascum plants but won't kill them. © Jean Vernon.

How to spot

You can't miss the giant blimp-like caterpillars feeding on verbascum, figwort and sometimes buddleia. They grow quickly into large, segmented, Pillsbury characters, with fat legs that grip and climb through the foliage. If you use a light trap you may find the brown adult moths that fly in April and May.

How to attract

Plant verbascum and if you live in southern counties of the UK, they will come. These pretty perennials are very garden worthy, flowering for weeks in the garden, but there are also some wildflower species that are common in nature such as great mullein that grows in calcareous wasteland and rough grassland. It's an important pollinator plant and a vital larval plant for Mullein moths. But it also provides fluff for the Wool Carder bee, which shaves the leaves to line her nests.

Elephant Hawk Moth (*Deilephila elpenor*)

The hawk moths are important pollinators and the Elephant Hawk moth is no exception. It's a common garden moth, though you might not realise it because it mostly flies at dusk when its food plants are strongly fragrant and rich in nectar. Adults feed on night-scented honeysuckle and hover while feeding. The olive green and pink markings are quite extraordinary; it's a great one to find for the kids.

Its caterpillars are just as dramatic because the grey ones look a bit like an elephant trunk, but there are green forms too. It's the trunk-like look that gave it its common name. They have huge black eyes near the head to scare off predators. When under attack they actually swell up, brandishing their fake eyes to complete the scary effect. The caterpillars feed on fuchsias, willow herbs, Himalayan balsam and bedstraws. There is a similar looking Small Elephant Hawk moth.

Possibly the most beautiful UK moth, the Elephant Hawk moth (Deilephila elpenor) is an absolute jewel. © Brigit Strawbridge-Howard.

How to spot

If you grow honeysuckle, you might find these beautiful moths feeding on the scented flowers at dusk from May to July. Go out at dusk and see what you can find. It's an amazing moth to show the youngsters.

The caterpillars are active and feeding from mid summer onwards and then pupate under the soil near their food plants. Look out for large elephant trunk-like caterpillars with prominent eyespots.

How to attract

Grow its caterpillar plants. The willow herbs are common garden 'weeds' and in a cottage garden are worthy fillers. There is a white form that is particularly pretty, though they do self seed and spread. Fuchsias are an important food plant and the caterpillars have been recorded on dahlias and lavender. They won't be present in huge numbers; the females lay one or two eggs at a time, so you don't risk losing your plants and the bonus is having these amazing moths in your garden.

MOTH TRAPS AND LEARNING MORE

Once you spark an interest in moths it gets a bit addictive. It doesn't take too much effort to get outside and start to spot these amazing creatures and other pollinators in and around your garden. If you can team up with a moth enthusiast you will learn loads. See if there is a moth night near you or tune into a moth expert or two on social media; you will be amazed at how fascinating these creatures are.

Join in with Moth Night (Ref 53). Or invest in a light trap and a good book to get you started. Lights are very good for attracting moths. The problem with mothing is that you have to wait until 10 o'clock at night when the sun goes down, as the best mothing time is June/July and August. So the best way to show the moths to children is to get a special moth trap and put that out so that the moths will be in the trap next day. That way the children get to see the beautiful moths without having to stay up all night.

Or have a go with treacling in a woodland where you can see what species are attracted to your fruity sweet concoction. Moth enthusiast and naturalist Mark Spencer gave me this recipe. Mix black treacle with brown sugar and a good beer, heat gently in a saucepan until dissolved and then pour into a jar and allow to cool. At dusk add a measure of rum and using a paintbrush paint it onto trees trunks or fence posts. Then go out with a torch to see which moths have been attracted to the delicious scents of alcohols and sugar.

Bees

If you were asked to name a pollinator the chances are the first thing that comes to mind are the bees. Quite possibly you would envisage the honeybee or maybe you might think of our lovely bumblebees.

I am a bit addicted to bees so condensing the bees into a few pages is going to be a real challenge. But if you want to learn more, my best-selling first book *The Secret Lives of Garden Bees* is a good partner book to this one.

Bees come in all shapes and sizes. You may be very surprised to learn that there are bees the size of a grain of rice and some which are as big as a small apricot. What is even more amazing is that within the islands and highlands of the United Kingdom, there are somewhere in the region of 275 different types of bee. Some are more common than others, but there are a fair few of these bees

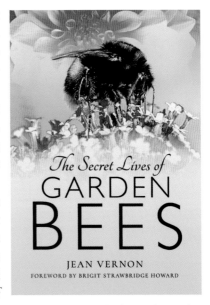

Learn more about garden bees with Jean's first book: The Secret Lives of Garden Bees.

that are probably living and breathing in your garden. And they are all pollinators so that's great for the plants and for anyone growing food crops that need this special service to produce seed, fruit, pods, nuts and berries. Bees are also a vital layer of the food chain, the cycle of nature and the intricate entangled web of biodiversity.

HONEYBEES

Many people are shocked to learn that the honeybee is just one species of the 275 bees in the UK. It is the only species of bee in the UK that makes honey as we know it. The honey is made from nectar collected from flowers and is concentrated down into the winter food that is stored in honeycomb within the nest. Honeybees also mix pollen with honey and ferment this to create something that is called beebread.

Honeybees are rightly revered and they do an important service as pollinators, but surprisingly there are other bees that are much better at pollination. Keeping honeybees will not save the bees. If you simply want to improve your fruit crop, or get better pollination then concentrate on helping the wild bees; it's much easier than keeping honeybees and the wild bees are excellent pollinators. Whatever you do to support all the pollinators will benefit the honeybees too.

Honeybees are generally 'farmed' by hobby beekeepers and commercial beekeepers for a number of high value and hugely cherished products.

HONEY

Honey is the golden nectar that the honeybees make from flower nectar, flower essences and many other medicinal components that they forage for in and around our gardens.

Honey is their winter food. Honeybees spend all summer collecting the nectar, processing it into honey and then storing it inside perfect hexagonal cells made out of bees wax. By the time the weather draws in and winter arrives a healthy honeybee colony should have enough stores to last it through winter and into spring. The honey that they make is more than their food. It is their medicine too: a bee panacea made from flowers that fires their whole essence and existence and contains everything that they need to be healthy.

Honeybees visit two million flowers and fly 50,000 miles to produce one pound of the amber nectar. It takes 12 honeybees to make a teaspoon of honey in their lifetime.

Honey is a miraculous creation. It doesn't go off and has very powerful healing powers. So instead of pouring it over our cereal or spreading it thickly on toast, we too should regard it as a medicine and use it respectfully.

Honeybees also make beeswax, which they use to build comb, not just for storing honey but also to house their larvae as they grow from egg to bee. The wax is secreted between scales on their body and then used to build extraordinary sheets of perfect comb. Honeybees also make propolis from tree resin and other plant ingredients. They use it to plug gaps around their hive. Beekeepers call it bee glue, but it is also highly revered for its medicinal qualities.

Honeybees are a common garden visitor, on heleniums. © Martin Mulchinock.

ATTRACTING GARDEN POLLINATORS

GARDEN BUMBLEBEES

Our gardens come alive with bumblebees in the spring. Most gardeners will be aware of two or three different sorts of bumblebee visiting their gardens. But in fact there are seven or eight species that are commonly seen in many gardens and another 16 or so that are much more rare. Identification is a bit of a dark art; some are much easier than others but there are a few that even the experts struggle to tell apart. To complicate matters the colouration of many bees, including bumblebees, fades in the spring and summer sunshine and there are always a few anomalies where a yellow band might be missing or a bee is black all over. The different castes of bumblebee, queen, worker, male, each have different markings, so determining exactly which bumblebee is feeding on your flowers can be a challenge. But it's fun and you will learn more about these enigmatic creatures. If you are really keen you can join a bumblebee identification course with the Bumblebee Conservation Trust or a similar group. In the meantime here are a few to look out for.

GARDEN BUMBLEBEE (*BOMBUS HORTORUM*)

Gardeners have their very own bumblebee, *Bombus hortorum* (think horticulture), more commonly known as the Garden bumblebee. It is a familiar species in our gardens and it is also a fairly easy bumblebee to identify.

This bee has a long face, (think horse/hortorum) and possibly the longest tongue of all bumblebees, up to 1.5cm. It's so long that the bee can often be seen with its tongue extended, such that it looks like a unicorn as it flies, ready to poke it into long tubular flowers. This species is slimmer than some of the other bumblebees. The Garden bumblebee has three yellow bands, but the third

Large bumblebees visiting foxgloves are most likely to be the Garden bumblebee (Bombus hortorum). © Jean Vernon.

band is at the base of its thorax (backpack) and there is another at the top of the abdomen, so sometimes these two bands look like one thick band, giving the bee a two yellow band appearance. Look carefully, especially if the bee has the characteristic long face. Check out its favourite flowers. If you've got bumblebees feeding on your foxgloves the chances are they are the Garden bumblebee.

The long tongue does restrict which flowers this bee can feed from and so it is also a common sight on salvias, comfrey, lavender, viper's bugloss, nasturtiums, honeysuckle, dead nettles, penstemon and clematis, where it can safely poke in its tongue to soak up nectar.

This bumblebee makes shallow nests in the garden and can choose odd places to set up home, like a coat pocket in the shed.

FOXGLOVE TRAFFIC CONTROL

For the best genetic diversity, plants need cross-pollination, and that means pollen from the flowers of another plant to fertilise its ovules. It is the pollinators that move the pollen from plant to plant, but some plants, like the foxglove, have evolved to reduce pollination from their own flowers and encourage cross-pollination (Ref 6). Foxgloves achieve this by loading the female flowers that form at the base of the flower stalk with more nectar. The flowers also have hairs inside to prevent smaller insects from stealing the nectar without pollinating the flowers. It is the Garden bumblebee that is its most frequent visitor and probably its most effective pollinator. These bees can detect the higher nectar density in the flowers at the base of the flower spike, so they visit these female flowers first, bringing pollen from other foxgloves. They will then work their way up the flower towards the top male flowers, which have lower nectar rewards but lots of pollen. This means that they only collect pollen from this plant at the very top, just as they are about to leave it and fly off to find a fresh foxglove. This one-way flow of bee traffic and pollen redistribution helps the foxgloves avoid inbreeding.

White-Tailed Bumblebee (*Bombus lucorum agg*)

The queen bees of the White-tailed bumblebee are early emerging, large bees with white tails and more lemony yellow bands on the thorax than the other early emerger, the Buff-tailed bumblebee. There are three forms of this species in the UK, though you are pretty unlikely to tell them apart by sight. Experts use DNA testing to distinguish

ATTRACTING GARDEN POLLINATORS

White bottomed queen bees with lemon yellow stripes are usually White-tailed bumblebees (Bombus lucorum agg.) © Jean Vernon.

between *Bombus lucorum* and the similar sub species *Bombus cryptarum* and *Bombus magnus*. Its short-tongue means that it can't feed from long tubular flowers, instead favouring shorter flowers with accessible nectar and pollen. But these naughty bees are also nectar robbers and will bite holes in the base of flowers such as comfrey, salvias and other longer tubular flowers and soak up nectar through these holes, because their tongues are too short to actually reach the nectar by the front door. It's a very clever adaptation and doesn't seem to affect the efficacy of pollination of the plants in general. These bees also nest in old rodent nests, such as mouse and vole holes.

The Red-Tailed Bumblebee (*Bombus lapidarius*)

One of the easiest garden bumblebees to identify is the Red-tailed bumblebee. This beautiful dark bumblebee has a rich red/orange bottom. The queen bees and workers have mostly black bodies. The male bees have the distinctive red bottom and yellow facial hair and also a yellow thorax. This is a widespread, short-tongued bumblebee and it often appears to have a preference for yellow flowers (Ref 6). The queen bees emerge in March and April and often nest in old rodent holes and stonewalls.

The distinctive red bottom is a tell-tale sign you've got the Red-tailed bumblebee (Bombus lapidarius) in your garden. © Jean Vernon.

The Buff-Tailed Bumblebee (*Bombus terrestris*)

Look out for these loud, unmistakable, fluffy flying golf balls whizzing around the garden searching for nectar and pollen. These are the queens of the beautiful Buff-tailed bumblebee and they are some of the largest bumblebees you will see in your garden. Queens emerge early in February in favourable conditions. They have the distinctive buffish-beige tail tip; the workers and the males of this species have white bottoms which makes them difficult to distinguish from the White-tailed bumblebees in summer. This is another naughty bee. Its short tongue restricts its diet to open accessible and short corolla flowers, but it has learnt to rob the long tubular flowers by chewing holes above the nectary on the flowers and poking its tongue through the hole to soak up the nectar. It nests in old vole and mouse holes, usually underground (hence its scientific name *terrestris* – meaning 'of the earth/land') and is also known to make nests under garden sheds and in compost heaps/bins.

*Worker Buff-tailed bumblebees (*Bombus terrestris*) have more golden orange bands and usually a white tail, seen here on knapweed. © Jean Vernon.*

THE GINGER BEES

There are four bumblebees that are sometimes referred to as the ginger bees. The most common one is the Common Carder bee (*Bombus pascuorum*), which you will undoubtedly find in your garden. But there are three other ginger bumblebees

you just might be lucky enough to come across, though they are very hard to tell apart because there are huge variations in their colouring. The rarer species include the Brown-banded Carder bee (*Bombus humilis*), the Moss Carder bee (*Bombus muscorum*) and the very rare Shrill Carder bee (*Bombus sylvarum*). These bees make shallow nests in mossy mounds, grassy tussocks and shallow hollows, and 'card' grass and fibres to form a nest. They are small bumblebees with longer tongues. They emerge a little later than other species in April and May and usually remain active much later in the season than other bumblebees, when they need plenty of late flowering forage.

Look out for the lovely Common Carder bee (Bombus pascuorum). It has a long tongue and loves comfrey. © Jean Vernon.

Tree Bumblebee (*Bombus hypnorum*)

Have you ever had bumblebees nesting in a bird box? Or under the house eaves? If you have I could almost guarantee that they were Tree bumblebees. And that's because this little bee needs a hollow space up high to nest. It would normally nest in a hollow tree, but these are a rare commodity. The queens move vertically when looking for a nesting

The Tree bumblebee (Bombus hypnorum) is a pretty bumblebee with a white bottom and a gingery thorax. © Jean Vernon.

place and find empty bird boxes. They have even been known to eject nesting birds! It's a pretty little bee with a ginger backpack and a white tail. It's been in the UK since about 2001 and has spread widely. In mid summer when the male bees have hatched the nest will get very busy, almost boiling over with activity as they wait to woo and date the new virgin queens.

How to Attract Bumblebees

Grow lots of early flowering plants including spring bulbs like crocuses and grape hyacinths. Extend the foraging season with late flowering plants to enable the new queens to build up their fat reserves in late summer and early autumn to survive winter. Anything you can do in your garden to help the bees will support bumblebees.

Allow moss to grow and leave a little bit of the garden wild so that beneficial plants like brambles, dandelions and willow herb can grow.

Let the wildflowers in the lawn grow and flower. Many bumblebees feed on clover, self-heal, bird's foot trefoil, dandelions, thistles and daisies. Leave north-facing banks undisturbed from late summer until spring; these are the preferred spots for many overwintering queen bumblebees. The winter sun won't reach the bank until spring, so it stops them waking on sunny winter days.

HELP! I'VE GOT A BUMBLEBEE NEST!

Bumblebees do nest in gardens and often under sheds, in compost bins or in bird boxes. The colonies don't usually live more than three or four months so think carefully about whether they are really doing any harm and see if you can live with them until their cycle is complete. Bumblebees rarely sting. They have an important role in pollinating plants and add to the rich biodiversity of your garden.

CUCKOO BEES

Cuckoo bumblebees are real bees and some of them, formerly classified as *Psithyrus* (bumblebee cuckoo bees) have an uncanny knack of looking just like the bee species that they parasitise.

Just like their namesake, the cuckoo, these bees lay their eggs in another bee's nest. The cuckoo bee enters the nest and kills or displaces the host queen bee. She then lays her eggs in the nest and enslaves the worker bees, so that they raise her offspring.

There are six species of cuckoo bumblebees that you may find in your garden, which parasitise specific species of bumblebee. As the cuckoo bumblebees use a

MEET THE POLLINATORS

host to raise their young they don't have worker bees and they don't collect pollen so the pollen baskets are missing. Look out for nectaring bees, with dark wings on your garden plants.

Solitary bees also have cuckoo bee species that parasitise their nests, but unlike the bumblebee cuckoos they don't generally look like their hosts. So for example some of the nomad bees, of which there are around 30 UK species, look a bit like wasps. They lay their eggs in the nests of some of the mining bees (*Andrena spp*), and their larvae feed on the food provided for each egg by the solitary bee host; some eat the larvae too. And of course this means the solitary bees won't emerge in spring but the cuckoo bees will instead.

The common Vestal cuckoo bee (Bombus vestalis) resembles and parasitises the nests of the Buff-tailed bumblebees. © Jean Vernon.

Cuckoo bees are real bees and are an important part of the biodiversity and have a role to play. There needs to be a healthy population of the host bees for the cuckoos to survive so it's a good sign when the cuckoos are present.

The Marsham's Nomad bee is a cleptoparasite of some Andrena mining bees, on apple blossom. © Jean Vernon.

ATTRACTING GARDEN POLLINATORS

SOLITARY BEES

The solitary bees are the unsung heroes of the garden and in many cases they are much better pollinators than the honeybees. I prefer to call these bees the 'Indie' bees, because they are mostly very independent. Well, at least the females are. It's a harsh world for the female solitary bees. In simplest terms they are like the single mums of the bee world. The males of each species usually emerge first and dissipate, staking out the nests or common forage plants so that when the females emerge they are set upon by eager males, they mate, and then the real work begins. There are around 250 different species of solitary bee in the UK, which is quite incredible. It's the females that make a nest, often intricate, with separately lined cells for each egg, which are provisioned with protein rich pollen and nectar to sustain the hatching larva before it pupates into an adult.

Flower Bees

You would think because all bees feed from flowers that they could all be called flower bees, but there is a small group of five species of bees called the flower bees. One of my favourites is the bumblebee-like Hairy-footed Flower bee, the males have feathery legs. This little beauty is one of the earliest garden bees to emerge, sometimes as early as February, and is usually around until midsummer. In the bee world it is the species that heralds the start of spring, emerging when the early spring flowers are starting to blossom. If you live in the southern half of the UK there's a good chance you will see this bee in your garden, especially in gardens with a rich diversity of spring flowers in abundance.

It's a type of solitary bee, and has a few favourite plants that it visits for food, one of which is the early flowering lungwort where it

Gingery male Hairy-footed Flower bees (Anthophora plumipes) feed on garden lungwort. © Gail Ashton.

can be found flitting very fast from flower to flower as it feeds. It's an accomplished aerial acrobat and skilled at hovering, resembling a little hummingbird in its mode of action and about the size of a bumblebee. It is pretty difficult to photograph because it moves so fast, but that actually helps in identification of this species. If you've got a decent patch of lungwort in flower there's a good chance you'll get the Hairy-footed Flower bee visiting. It's widespread, but more common in south and eastern England and records are gradually increasing further north too, but it is currently unknown in Ireland and Scotland.

The female, who only mates once, is choosy in her choice of parent for her babies. So the male Hairy-footed Flower bee has to work hard and perform a few acrobatic manoeuvres to win her heart, but he has a surprising bedside manner to add to the equation. Before the courtship, the male not only hangs in the air to get her attention, but he has to move fast to gain his prize before his competitors move in. But while in the act of mating, the male appears to massage her eyes with his feathery front legs.

These bees nest in burrows excavated in compacted clay banks, old cobb walls, soft mortar, cavities in soft cliff faces, clay soil and even around weathered chimneystacks. The nests are usually quite shallow, but the bees can nest *en masse*, giving the appearance of a social species, when in fact they are an abundance of solitary bees nesting in aggregation. At RHS Wisley in Surrey there is a population of these bees nesting in a cobb wall, which now has an information board alerting visitors to their presence and welcoming these precious pollinators.

How to spot
Stake out a clump of lungwort or a patch of primroses in spring and watch out for these very fast flying bees flitting from flower to flower. They emerge from late February onwards. The gingery males, with a paler creamy face and feathery legs emerge first and then the dark females hatch and start to feed.

How to attract
Plant early spring flowering plants like primroses, comfrey and especially lungwort and deadnettles. Make cobb bricks for nesting sites from clay and straw and sand.

Mining Bees

Many of our solitary bees make their nests in the ground and are grouped together as mining bees. Our largest group of mining bees is the Andrena genus, but there are a few others. These bees need exposed bare ground, especially sandy soil patches where they can excavate their nests and make little underground caves to lay their eggs. Look out for volcano shaped piles of soil: these are called tumuli, and may be seen

ATTRACTING GARDEN POLLINATORS

The Ashy mining bee (Andrena cineraria) has distinctive colouring and a panda like look. © Gail Ashton.

in close mown lawns or banks of sandy soil. These are the excavation piles that the female bee makes as she burrows in the ground. Mining bees don't use the bee houses that some gardeners like to place in their gardens. Instead they choose closely mown lawns, bare patches of soil in sunny places and sometimes between paving slabs in the garden. Mining bees like most other solitary bees don't sting, which makes them great to show the kids and help them to appreciate wild bees. There are about 70 different species of mining bee in the UK. Most belong to the Andrena family and include the black and grey panda-like Ashy Mining bee which is common and another great bee to show the children.

How to spot

Look out for bees excavating the soil in your garden. They make neat little mounds of sandy soil like mini volcanoes, but will seal the holes in bad weather and at night to protect them and their nests. Mining bees will gather nectar and pollen from your garden flowers and then use these to provision every egg that they lay in their nests. Mining bees tend to collect pollen on their legs, but not like honeybees and bumblebees that have obvious panniers packed with pollen, like fat blobs on their hind legs. Instead the mining bees gather the pollen and groom it onto hairs on their legs.

How to attract

Leave bare areas of soil in your garden, especially in sunny places or well-drained sandy soil. Mow parts of your lawn tight and mow after dusk when the bees are less active and hunkered down in their nests. If you already have mining bees in your garden then keep doing what you are doing: the bees like it!

The Ivy Bee (*Colletes hederae*)

Before you strip the wild ivy from your garden extremities spare a thought for the Ivy bee. This solitary bee feeds almost exclusively on the flowers of wild ivy. It's a fairly recent addition to the UK's bee fauna and our only true autumnal bee. The Ivy bee is a solitary bee that was first recorded in the UK in 2001 having arrived from Europe. The freshly emerging bees appear in September just as the wild ivy is in flower, providing the Ivy bees and many other pollinators with essential pollen and nectar in this late point of the season. They are ground nesting bees that build nests in suitable soil; the eggs mature and pupate underground before the adults start emerging in September.

How to spot

Ivy bees may be seen *en masse* flying fast over the soil, seemingly together in social behaviour, but while they can be present in large numbers these are actually individual bees going about their business, seeking food and mating partners in the short time that the ivy is in flower. These bees are quite strikingly stripy with very distinct yellow and dark brown stripes on their bodies.

How to attract

Let the ivy grow and flower. It's a very important autumn food source for many of our precious pollinators.

Avoid digging over areas of soil where you know these bees to be nesting. And always leave an area of soil undisturbed in any garden to ensure any mining bees can develop underground.

You can report sightings of the Ivy bee as part of a BWARS (Bees, Wasps & Ants Recording Society) citizen science project that is plotting the spread of this bee in the UK (See the 'Learning More' section at the end of this book.)

If you see a very stripy bee in early autumn it could be the Ivy bee (Colletes hederae), here on ivy. © Liam Olds.

Leaf-Cutter Bees (*Megachile spp*)

The leaf-cutter bees are a group of solitary bee species that most gardeners are familiar with, mostly because these bees leave tell tale signs all around the garden that they are alive and active. There are eight UK species of leaf-cutter bees and once you get to recognise these cute little bees you will see more and more of them around your garden. These solitary bees rarely sting and go about their business in your garden with little regard for human activity. They are simply fascinating to observe.

Leaf-cutter bees cut circular and semi circular sections out of garden leaves, most commonly roses, but other leaves of other smooth leaved trees and shrubs can also be used, such as sycamore and lilac.

She (it's always the females that do the work and nest building) stands on the leaf and cuts around her body and then flies off with the leaf segment to seal her egg chambers. Leaf-cutter bees do not eat the leaves of your plants and they are not garden pests. Plants and leaves that have had the leaf-cutter bee treatment are not harmed or injured in any way and there is really no need to worry about your plants. Never, ever try and control them or treat them as a pest, they are an absolute joy. Plants affected will simply grow more leaves in due course. In fact it is a real pleasure to see the notches around the garden because it means these exceptional creatures are alive and well. The leaf-cutter bees are excellent pollinators, better than honeybees. This is because they are messy little bees and manage to get completely covered in pollen as they forage for food. They have a hairy underbelly designed to trap the pollen and as they move from flower to flower they transport the pollen grains to the female flower parts and pollination occurs.

Leaf-cutter bees prefer to nest in existing cavities, which makes them another of the bee species that are likely to nest in a bee

Look out for the tell-tale signs of Leaf-cutter bees in the garden. These cute bees make swaddling clothes out of plant leaves and petals. © Jean Vernon.

You can see the orange feathery scopa underneath this Leaf-cutter bee. © Jean Vernon.

hotel or insect house. They will also nest in the ground and some will even nest in neglected plant pots. Each nest will contain about six individual cells and every one is supplied with a mix of pollen and nectar to feed the larva when it hatches out. The female eggs are positioned at the back of the nest and the males, which emerge first, are positioned at the front.

The leaf-cutter bee actually lines the cavity with pieces of leaf or sometimes flower petals and seals each cell with a leafy cap. Uncovered or excavated they look like mini cigars.

How to spot

Look out for little notches cut out of the leaves of garden shrubs but especially roses and azaleas. These are the signs that the Leaf-cutter bees are nesting nearby.

Keep an eye on pollen rich garden flowers, which these bees will visit to gather pollen to provision each egg that they lay. They are fascinating to watch and quite messy in their activity and are usually well dusted with pollen.

If you have a bee house or insect hotel it is often leaf-cutter bees that populate the nesting tubes. Watch out for activity around May or June when the females may start to nest. They seal each egg chamber and the face of the nesting tube with a piece of leaf so they are quite easy to spot. They will also nest in natural cavities, hollow stems and other watertight narrow tubes.

How to attract

Plant more pollen rich open flowers that are in flower in mid to late summer.

Grow more roses and shrubs to provide more nesting material.

The Wool Carder Bee (*Anthidium manicatum*)

The Wool Carder bee gets its name from its nest building activities. The females shave the woolly hairs off plant stems to line their nest cells and lamb's ears is one of the plants it does this to. Its perfect bunny ear shaped leaves are just covered in soft grey fur, well it's not fur of course, it is dense leaf hairs that the plants use to protect its leaves from intense sunshine and reduce evaporation at the leaf surface. But the whorls of its soft pink flowers are also a good source of nectar and it is in established clumps of this plant where you can often find these bees in summer. The Wool Carder bee is widespread in the UK but its distribution in more northern regions is less clear.

The Wool Carder bee is a common garden bee; it is quite dark in appearance with yellow spots down the sides of the abdomen and yellow markings on the face and on the legs.

The males are larger than the females and are very territorial. They will stake out a prime feeding spot waiting for a female and defend their patch from other males and other large insects including bumblebees and hoverflies. The males will literally chase off other bees of other species in their quest to find their mate. The males have spiky spines at the tip of their abdomen and brandish them like weapons when defending their territory. The female bee collects pollen to provision her eggs on her underside, collecting the grains between the rear facing hairs underneath her. Like the leaf-cutter bee, this makes them excellent pollinators as they move pollen from flower to flower.

How to spot
These bees are on the wing in the summer months, usually between June and August. You might see them nesting in a bee hotel, though that is fairly rare.

The Wool carder bee (Anthidium manicatum) has a favourite garden plant. The males guard lamb's ears (Stachys byzantina) in hope of meeting females there. © Gail Ashton.

Look out for the female bees taking the fluff from hairy plants such as lamb's ears and other stachys species.

On a warm summers day spend some time watching a clump of lamb's ears for this bee's unique behaviour. Look out for the aggressive territorial behavior by the male Wool Carder bee.

How to attract

Grow the food plants that this species needs – mints, toadflax, vetches and legumes as well as generous clumps of lamb's ear.

Carpenter Bees

Carpenter bees are generally bees that make nests in wood, tunnelling into stems or using beetle holes. We have an extraordinary bee that is occasionally seen in the UK called the Violet Carpenter bee, but it is a summer visitor and not believed to breed here. The other UK bee that is regarded as a carpenter bee is the Campanula bee, also called the Harebell Carpenter bee and is truly the smallest UK bee, measuring just a few millimeters (5–6mm) in length. It is very small and doesn't really look like what most people think a bee should look like. It looks more like a long-bodied

The tiny black Campanula bee feeds pretty much exclusively on campanula pollen. © Val Bourne.

black fly. Also as it's so small it is often overlooked as being a bee, even though it can be a frequent visitor to many gardens. This small, slender black bee can be found in gardens from midsummer until the middle of August, predominantly in southern England. It's so tiny in fact that unless you are looking for it, you may not even see it.

Clusters of male Campanula bees can congregate around open campanula flowers in summer. If you have campanula flowers in your garden, look out for male Campanula bees overnighting and huddled together inside the flowers, especially in dull, damp weather. Campanula bees usually mate inside the flowers, so when a female arrives to collect pollen, she will have the undivided attention of several males and will likely mate successfully in the pretty blue bell shaped flowers. This little bee needs a special group of plants to survive. It feeds on the pollen and nectar from harebells (campanulas), mostly the ones that are called the nettle leaved and clustered bellflower, both are popular garden plants. Some campanulas grow wild (especially the true harebell). These bees are also known to feed on the nectar of some hardy geraniums. It's the female that collects the pollen by landing inside the flowers. She grips the pollen-laden anthers between her mandibles and her front legs and her back legs push the dusty white pollen back so that the grains are stored in the pollen-collecting hairs under her abdomen. Females are also known to rub their abdomen against the pollen-laden anthers. She will use this pollen to provide food for her eggs that she lays in tiny woodworm holes and dry, thin hollow stems. The males simply feed on nectar, mostly from campanulas but also sometimes from hardy geraniums.

How to spot
If you live in southern counties and you have campanulas in your garden then stake them out from mid to late summer and you just might be lucky. But remember this bee is very small, black and more ant-like than bee-like.

How to attract
The Campanula bee will make a nest in woodworm holes, so leave rotting tree stumps and worm riddled fence posts *in situ* for it to make a safe nest for its babes. It is so tiny that the tubes and hollows in bee boxes and bee houses are too big and wide for this species. Make a bundle of dry reeds, chive stems and grasses, trimmed with their ends revealed, and place in a sheltered, dry tube as alternative nesting sites.

This tiny bee needs mud to seal its egg chambers, so a muddy/puddled area with wet soil provides the essential mud needed to assist its nesting activity. A source of mud near to nests means the bees expend less vital energy searching for and gathering this material.

Mason Bees (*Osmia spp*)

The mason bees are some of the most common solitary garden bee species. They nest in cavities and if you install a bee house or a bee box you will undoubtedly get these bees nesting inside. The most well-known of the eleven UK species is the Red Mason bee, though it is scarcer in Scotland and Ireland. It is an extraordinary pollinator, with one mason bee pollinating more flowers than a staggering 120 honeybees. Instead of collecting pollen on its legs the mason bee has a hairy underside of its abdomen and stores the pollen there. This makes it an excellent pollinator, because the pollen will brush over the flower's stigmas as the bee feeds. It's also very fond of fruit tree nectar, so if you need better pollination of apples, pears and other spring flowering trees, mason bees offer a fantastic pollination service and are a better choice for gardens than a honeybee hive.

Like most solitary bees mason bees don't sting, which means you can get up close with children. And Red Mason bees are available to buy as cocoons so you could actually buy them, hatch them and watch them fly off into your garden. What a lovely project for youngsters. Alternatively invest in some special mason bee tubes and install them in a special nesting bee box, protecting the front with a predator guard to deter woodpeckers and other opportunists. You can replace the tubes each year to keep your nester free from pests and parasites.

Red mason bees (Osmia bicornis), are excellent pollinators and seal their nests with mud. © Liam Olds.

How to spot

The Red Mason bee is on the wing from April to June, but sometimes as early as March. Look out for it gathering nectar and pollen from spring blossom, especially fruit trees. You might also find it collecting mud or nesting in a garden bee house. The females have a distinctive red fluffy abdomen, though this can fade, and black heads. The antennae curve inwards, which is unusual in solitary bees.

How to attract

Set up nesting tubes in a suitable bee nester in the garden. Leave a mud patch or puddle so that there is plenty of material for these bees to seal their egg cells. Plant lots of spring flowering plants, but especially apples and pears. You will get a great crop of fruit and help the bees too.

FUNNY BEE BEHAVIOUR

Bees are quite incredible. The more you think you know the more you discover. Here are a few fun facts about bees. If you want to learn more you might like my other book: *The Secret Lives of Garden Bees*.

High Five

Bumblebees rarely sting, but like a dog giving a warning growl before it bites, the bumblebee has a quirky little move it makes to ward off attack. Get too close to a bumblebee and it might raise a back leg. It's not a high-five, it means back off. I often see it when trying to take a photo, and now it makes me smile. Don't mess with bees!

Not All Bees Can Sting

Many of the solitary bees don't sting at all, that makes them safe for children. It is the female egg laying apparatus that has evolved into a stinger, which means that male bees can't and don't sting. Bumblebee males often have yellow moustaches and facial hair, which is a useful way to tell them apart. They don't have pollen baskets either!

Children love to know that some male bees have facial hair like this Early bumblebee (Bombus pratorum)*. © Jean Vernon.*

Bee Vision

Bees perceive colours differently to us, they have extrasensory powers, or at least their sight is within the UV spectrum which makes red look black. Look at the colour of the flowers the bees like best in your garden, Some research suggests that purple flowers, often the preferred colour of many bees, have more nectar, with blue flowers a close second. There is also some evidence that suggests flowers and flower colour have evolved to suit the colour vision of the native bees. UV light also highlights floral nectar guides, directing the bees to the sugary prize in their nectaries.

Look for the floral guides on flower petals signalling towards the nectary. © Jean Vernon.

Electric Attraction (Pollen magnet)

The fluffy nature of some bees literally attracts pollen to them as they forage; even the male bees will have a light pollen dusting despite not actively collecting pollen. As they move from flower to flower these minute grains are brushed past and onto the sticky stigmas of other flowers.

But it seems that there's some other fascinating bee–flower interactions going on, revolving around a flower's electric aura. Researchers from the University of Bristol (Ref 7) discovered, by using fake electrified flowers, that bumblebees can actually perceive the electrical field around a flower. They also discovered that the bees seemed to be able to tell which flowers had recently been visited (and the pollen collected or nectar supped) and move on to flowers that were unvisited, all through interpreting the electrical fields and the messages they conveyed. It is almost like a note on the door telling the bee whether the flower is open for business or not. There is also research that shows bees scent mark flowers as they forage.

Daylight Robbery

Naturalist Charles Darwin was possibly the first person to observe nectar robbing by short and medium-tongued humble-bees (as he called bumblebees) (Ref 8).

When flowers are scarce the shorter tongued bees will chew holes into long flowers to access the nectar because their tongues are too short to reach inside otherwise. © Jean Vernon.

In 1841 in a letter to *Gardener's Chronicle* (Ref 9) Darwin wrote about 'the humble-bees which bore holes in flowers, and thus extract the nectar', and speculated about this behaviour as an example of acquired knowledge in insects (Ref 10). He observed the behaviour on his garden salvias and penstemons. In essence, the shorter-tongued bumblebees, including the Buff-tailed and the White-tailed have developed this devious behaviour. You have to forgive them because when they emerge they need every drop of nectar they can find, and when it's at the base of a long tubular flower, their short tongues cannot reach it. So they chew holes into the base of the flower just above the nectaries. Take a look at the longer, tubular flowers in the garden and you may see the holes. It's a common technique on salvias, antirrhinums and comfrey, which normally need a long-tongued bee to pollinate. The hole is perfectly positioned for the bee to reach inside with its tongue and soak up the nectar.

Forced into Flower

When the queen bumblebees emerge in spring there can be a dearth of forage available. Scientists have discovered that bumblebees damage the leaves of plants to stress plants into flowering earlier, so providing an earlier source of vital protein-rich pollen (Ref 11).

Wasps

You might wonder why on earth I am encouraging you to attract wasps into your garden. Far from being annoying, the yellow and black stripy creatures that bother you in the summer when you are trying to enjoy a picnic, a pint at the pub or a garden barbecue, wasps have lots of other very positive roles to play in the environment. If you take a little time to get to know a bit more about wasps, I am sure you will be fascinated.

Wasps are actually important pollinators and much more. Common wasp (Vespula vulgaris). © Gail Ashton.

Wasps are incredible garden pest control, they feed paralysed caterpillars to their young. © Gail Ashton.

First of all bees and wasps are VERY closely related. Bees actually evolved from wasps! And the two families do share some similarities.

Wasps are important pollinators. Just like bees, they visit flowers to sup nectar to fuel their activity and as a result they often transfer pollen from plant to plant effecting pollination.

Many wasps are an incredible pest control in the garden. Wasps feed grubs and other insects to their larvae. This means they will take caterpillars, aphids and other insects from your garden, acting as a very effective biological pest control. It is estimated that the social wasps in the UK consume in total 14 million kilogrammes of insect prey every summer (Ref 12).

So just imagine the world without wasps!

What's more there are several forms of the social wasps that frequent our gardens and an astonishing estimated 7,000 different species of wasps within the United Kingdom. The variety of these insects is quite incredible and once you get over your fear of wasps and actually start to explore their diversity and understand their lifecycles, you will be simply amazed.

Wasps Galore

But it's not just the social wasps that frequent our gardens. Just like the bees, the wasp family includes solitary wasps that rely on a single female wasp to mate and then make a nest where she lays her eggs and provides a food source for the developing larvae. It's a very similar life cycle to many solitary bees and just as fascinating when you start to look into it all.

GREENHOUSE ALLIES

It's not just the social wasps that feed on some of the insects that we regard as pests in the garden. There are parasitic wasps that are now 'manufactured' in great numbers to be released inside glasshouses and polytunnels to control greenhouse whitefly and other insects that infest commercial crops and indeed our own homegrown tomatoes. It's a natural way to deal with problem insects without resorting to toxins and pesticides. There are even parasitic wasps that will control clothes moths and food moths inside the home. These wasps may not be pollinators, but they are an important player in the ecosystem.

Social Wasps (*Vespinae spp*)

There are seven species of social wasps in the UK within three different genera. These are the ones that you invite to your picnics every time you open a bottle of squash or a can of fizzy pop.

The social wasps have a lifecycle very much like a bumblebee. Bees evolved from wasps and so there are many overlaps of behaviour between the families. Just like the social bees, the mated queen wasps overwinter as adults and emerge in spring to start building a nest. And just like the bumblebee queen who crafts her nest from wax, the queen wasp will start to build a papier-mâché citadel. To do this she harvests wood fibre from timber posts, garden furniture and old

Just like other pollinators adult wasps feed on nectar rich flowers. © Jean Vernon.

wood, which she masticates into a wet malleable material and creates a paper thin dome within which she lays her first eggs.

This first brood is all female workers. When they hatch into larvae they are fed by the queen, who will go out and forage for protein rich food for her babes. She fuels herself on sugar rich nectar, which she collects from spring flowers. Even queen wasps are pollinators. Once the larvae have pupated into adult workers and emerge, they take over, much like the worker bees in a bumblebee or honeybee colony. Again the worker wasps are important pollinators, collecting nectar to fuel their hunting forays. The adult wasps collect a wide range of caterpillars, aphids and other garden insects that might attack our garden plants. They use this prey to feed their siblings but feast on just nectar themselves. When the workers take this protein-rich food to the larvae, they receive a small amount of sweet secretion, almost as a reward. This sugary diet explains why wasps become a bit difficult in mid summer, because that is when the wasp nest has produced the male wasps to mate with the newly emerged virgin queens. The nest starts to run down, there are no more larvae to feed and the workers crave the sweet treat secreted from the larvae that they feed. As the garden fruit starts to ripen they start to bite into the soft skins and feast on the fruit within.

And as we humans start to enjoy the summer these black and yellow striped buzzers gatecrash our *al fresco* activities in search of their sugar fix.

Social wasps are also vital in the lifecycle of some of the hoverflies, especially Volucella species, which lay their eggs inside wasp nests and whose larvae survive as brood parasites.

In autumn, wasps are often attracted to ripening fruit as they look for a sugar fix. © Jean Vernon.

How to spot

Social wasps have a waist, and a bright lairy livery of yellow and black stripes. You might hear the wasp queens in early spring seeking out not just nectar-rich spring shrubs, but also stripping timber decking, sheds and fences of fibre to craft their nests. Look out for wasp activity under sheds, inside known cavities where they may make a nest.

How to attract

Try to love and let live. Wasps aren't the enemy we sometimes perceive. Yes they can and do sting and if you have an allergy you need to take great care. But we can live in harmony with wasps and they are a vital part of the food chain and garden biodiversity, not to mention great pollinators. One wasp nest can generate a dozen or more queen wasps but each one of these has to successfully mate, overwinter and build a nest, and in reality possibly only two or three will actually survive to do just that. You might find it hard to actively attract wasps into your garden but anything you do to support them will also help other pollinators. Plant more nectar-rich flowers. Invite the wasps to your picnics by placing a decoy pot of jam somewhere else and protect your summer drinks with pretty lids and fabric covers. If you are allergic then you may have to take more drastic measures, but otherwise try and find the beauty in these creatures that are so closely related to the bees that we revere.

HELP! I'VE GOT A WASPS' NEST!

If you find a wasp nest in or around your home and garden don't panic. The first thing to remember is that a wasp nest is only active for a short few months and it is very rarely reused year after year.

Unless the wasps are getting into your house and stinging people, it is better to allow the colony to go through its lifecycle and complete it rather than interfere, or destroy it.

If you do choose to employ a wasp control company you will have to pay for their services. Usually they use very powerful chemicals to destroy the nest and its occupants and there is always a risk of these pesticides persisting and potentially affecting other insects, including our beneficial insect friends.

If you can live with the nest and allow it to live out its life, it will diminish and die out in late summer or early autumn and become a distant memory, leaving your garden free of toxins, your conscience clear and your bank balance a little healthier too.

ATTRACTING GARDEN POLLINATORS

HORNETS (*VESPA SPP*)

You might be surprised to learn that hornets are a type of wasp. And like other wasps they are also pollinators. In the British Isles we have one fairly common hornet species, the large, majestic European hornet (*Vespa cabro*) that can be found in our gardens. Hornets like wasps get a bad press. But actually they are less aggressive than other social wasps and extremely beautiful and elegant. They live in a colony like bumblebees and other social wasps, and are pollinators too, visiting many flowers to collect nectar to sustain their activities. Hornets catch other insect prey to feed to their offspring. If you accidentally disturb a hornets nest then you are likely to be attacked by the worker hornets that will sting you in the same way as you would disturbing a bumblebee nest. But generally these are gentle giants.

Take photos to ensure your visitor is our European hornet and not the invasive Asian hornet (*Vespula velutina*). There is a very active campaign tracking and controlling the invasion of the Asian hornet within the UK. It is considered to be a potentially damaging predator of honeybees and also other pollinators like bumblebees and solitary bees. It is smaller than our native European hornet and has less yellow abdominal stripes, being more commonly dark brown with just one yellow segment and a dark velvety thorax. Please don't kill hornets because you think you've found an Asian hornet. Most hornets in the UK will most likely be the lovely European hornets. Instead take photos to aid identification and make a note of your location. If you are not very tech savvy then use What 3 Words to give you a site reference. If you really do think you've seen an Asian hornet in the UK please report your find online using the recording form at iRecord (Ref 13).

Most hornets you will see in your garden are the gentle, beautiful European hornets (Vespa cabro). © Jean Vernon.

Ruby-Tailed Wasp (*Chrysis ignita agg.*)

The first time I saw this creature I was amazed at its jewel like colouring. It's a shiny metallic blue with a red abdomen. I was actually watching some leaf-cutter bees making their nests. That should have been a clue. For this little beauty lays its eggs in the nests of solitary bees and its larvae hatch first and then eat the newly hatched bee larvae and their food. As a bee enthusiast this is a tough one, but it's important to remember that when you see this wasp around, it means your garden is a good place for solitary bees to nest and thrive. This cuckoo wasp cannot survive without a healthy host population, so take it as a compliment and pat yourself on the back for a job well done providing good nesting sites for your beloved bees.

It's a clever wasp that enters into the nest of a solitary bee and lays its eggs alongside the bee eggs. If the Ruby wasp gets caught in the act by the female solitary bee then the Ruby wasp is well equipped to resist attack. Her very tough exoskeleton protects her from attack and she has a hollow abdomen which also allows her to curl up into a ball to protect herself (Ref 14). So she has a good chance of success. Once the bee seals up the cells and the nest with eggs of both species in place, their work is done and the likely result is that the new Ruby wasp adults will emerge in spring next year. The adults also visit flowers for nectar and pollen and are important pollinators.

If you find the spectacular Ruby-tailed Wasp (Chrysis ignita agg), look to see where there are nesting solitary bees nearby. © Liam Olds.

How to spot

You can't miss this little beauty. It's a small wasp, about 10mm long with a metallic blue green head and thorax and a rich ruby red abdomen and is on the wing from April to September. You might find the females hanging around insect houses and bee boxes or anywhere that solitary bees are nesting. They are particularly fond of mason bee nests so you may find them on sunny walls or near mason bee nests.

How to attract

Everything you do to attract garden pollinators into your garden will also help and support this species and others like them. The adults visit flowers for nectar to fuel their activity and will also pick up pollen, which they will pass from flower to flower. There are some very rare species of the Ruby-tailed wasps, which can be difficult to identify or tell apart from the more common species. Even though these wasps do parasitise bee nests, they are an essential part of garden biodiversity and cannot exist without healthy populations of their hosts. Sometimes it's hard to accept the adversities of life but nature knows best.

NATURE'S POTTER

The more I learn about pollinators the more fascinating they become. I have a wish list of insects I have read about or even written about that I have yet to see, and one of these is the Heath Potter wasp (*Eumenes coarctatus*). But this is a rare wasp and you are very unlikely to have this species in your garden. I first read about these curious creatures in Brigit Strawbridge Howard's first book, *Dancing with Bees*. Her poetic description of her Potter wasp quest with entomologist and artist John Walters is one of my favourite chapters in her book. At her book launch I was fascinated to chat to John about this enigmatic creature. Why the fascination? Well because this small creature actually crafts

The Heath potter wasp (Eumenes coarctatus) crafts tiny mud urns and lays her eggs inside. © Brigit Strawbridge Howard.

miniature Grecian urns from mud that she attaches to the stems of heathers so that they hang at just the right angle to stop the rain filling them up. Inside these vessels the female wasp lays her eggs and provisions them, not with pollen, but with paralysed caterpillars to ensure that when the larvae hatch there is food for each one. The larvae pupate inside the urn and then emerge again as adults the following spring. The Potter wasp is rare so you are very unlikely to find it in your garden, but the very fact that there is a wasp that makes pots merits a mention in my book so that you too can marvel at the wonders of nature and hopefully start to see the beauty in wasps and other unlikely creatures too.

Ichneumonid Wasps

These little cuties are often rather comical looking with oversized antennae. They are sometimes called Darwin wasps because of the renewed efforts to unravel their evolution (Ref 15). Worldwide there are thought to be in the region of between 60 and

The tiny, lightweight Ichneumon wasps often feed on the airy heads of the apiaceae. © Jean Vernon.

100 thousand species. Fantastically diverse and almost always parasitoidic, in the UK they number somewhere in the region of 2,500 species (Ref 16).

Many of these elegant, and often gangly looking creatures feed on plants and are notable pollinators feeding predominantly on apiaceae (formerly umbellifers) and especially wild carrot and similar species of the genus.

There is a very useful guide from the Natural History Museum (Ref 17) but this is still a very diverse and complicated group of insects. There are 33 subfamilies so it is often left to the experts to identify. Tell-tale signs that you've found an Ichneumonid wasp are criss-cross veins over two pairs of wings. They have long antennae with 18 or more segments and a very narrow wasp waist. Females also have long ovipositors (for laying eggs). Take lots of photos if you can so you can try and get it identified later.

Unlike many parasitic insects these creatures actually kill their hosts. It's pretty gruesome. Eggs are laid on, in or near the correct species of butterfly, beetle, sawfly and moth larvae, and even other parasitoids such as other Ichneumons and Tachinid flies (Ref 18). The emerging Ichneumonid larvae eat them alive and emerge from the empty skin and then pupate into adults. It's the stuff of horror films, but it's probably going on in a garden near you every summer! It's also very risky business because any predator of the wasp's host will eat its offspring, if it finds a parasitised larva for its supper. For this reason their hosts often have other defences such as hairs or chemical deterrents. Despite their scary appearance most of these wasps can't sting and they are important pollinators. Many of them are predators of garden insects that we might regard as pest species, so they have important garden roles to play.

They can also use very interesting techniques to suppress the immune system of their host, using polyDNA viruses (with a double strand DNA). It's an otherworldly technique, where a special virus, thought to have evolved with the wasps, is injected with the wasp egg into the host larvae. It's a three way relationship between the parasitoid wasp, the caterpillar and the virus. When present the virus then infects the cells of the larval host and affects the caterpillar's immune system. (Ref 19). If the virus is absent, the immune system of the caterpillar kills the wasps egg. But with the virus, the genes of the virus control the caterpillar metabolism and the wasp egg survives, hatches and devours the caterpillar from inside.

How to spot

You may find these wasps feeding on umbellifers in the garden. Some are nocturnal and can be found in moth traps. Look out for clear winged insects with long bodies, large and long antennae and a very slim waist. They can be quite colourful in shades of orange, red, yellow and black. The females have super-extended ovipositors for laying eggs in particular places.

This cryptine Ichneumonid wasp is Ischnus inquisitorius, *a parasitoid of tortricid moth pupae.* © *Gail Aston/ID Gavin Broad.*

How to attract

These curious wasps will be attracted to suitable nectar plants in and around your garden, but each species will be searching out its host. By encouraging a healthy population of butterflies, moths, wood boring beetles and other insects with a larval stage your garden will become richer in the host species needed by each Ichneumonid wasp. Don't forget the right habitats too. Leave fallen wood to rot down; some Ichneumonid females actually bore into the wood with their egg laying apparatus (ovipositor) to reach wood boring beetle grubs inside.

Hoverflies

In America hoverflies have the prettier name of flower flies and actually that sums them up perfectly.

If you've started looking at the insects in your garden you will have seen hoverflies. You might even have confused some of them with bees. And that's really not surprising

*Common spotted Field Syrph (*Eupodes luniger*) is a frequent garden visitor and a striking hoverfly. © Gail Ashton.*

as many hoverflies are bee mimics, replicating the stripy yellow/black livery to fool predators into thinking they might sting. They can't and don't. Hoverflies have two wings and belong to the Diptera (means two wings), whereas bees have four wings and belong to the Hymenoptera (the fore and hind wings are connected together with hooks). Hoverflies belong to the family Syrphidae.

In the UK there are around 270 different species of hoverfly and many of these visit flowers. That's a similar amount to the bees and like the bees there is much variation.

Hoverflies hover, though some other flies can do that too. They also visit our garden flowers to feed on nectar and are especially common during summer when the bees are on the wing too.

Hoverflies are very important garden pollinators. Some describe them as the unsung heroes of the garden (Ref 54). With bees top of the agenda when it comes to pollination, the hoverflies are underrated and less understood but in fact have very vital roles to play in the garden, agriculture and in nature. So much so that the humble hoverfly is considered to be the second most important pollinator after the bees (Ref 55).

Many hoverflies have insectivorous larvae that devour garden aphids and other small invertebrates that some gardeners consider to be pests. Others feed on rotting wood and decaying vegetable matter, and the presence of a healthy population of hoverflies can be an environmental indicator of the health of the surrounding land.

But hoverflies are also an important layer in the food chain and many are food for our insectivorous birds, reptiles and amphibians and of course other predatory insects.

Like all of our insect pollinators, hoverflies have three main phases of their growth: egg, larval stage and adult. But the habitats needed for different larvae are variable. Some feed on live prey, while others are aquatic. The female chooses where to lay her eggs depending on the needs of her larvae. Aphid eating species usually lay the eggs near to aphid populations or on plants that are susceptible to aphid infestation. The larvae can't move too far so they need a food source close by when they hatch from their egg. It's a good idea to understand what hoverfly larvae look like so that you don't confuse them for 'pests' or try to remove them from your plants. The simplest cure for this compulsive disorder is to live and let live and simply observe whatever life you find in your garden and greenhouse and try and learn as much as you can.

HOVERFLY LAGOONS

It sounds glamorous but some hoverflies lay their eggs in what have been affectionately named hoverfly lagoons. I suspect it is subterfuge to trick parents into allowing their youngsters to build and keep little lagoons for the pretty hoverflies. It's a great ruse anyway. Because in fact hoverfly lagoons are stinky pots of rotting leaves and vegetation. But the good news is that they help and support some of our precious hoverfly pollinators.

Larvae of our most common hoverflies feed on dead and decaying matter. They can be found in ditches and puddles filled with rotting leaves and debris where they suck in fluids rich in microbes and breathe through a rat-tail breathing tube. The tails may be short and snorkel like or long and rat-tailed.

Children love searching through the rotting material looking for rat-tailed larvae within the debris. Finally they can look out for the adults, some of which are affectionately called Batman hoverflies, due to their very distinctive markings. These are one of the most numerous and common hoverflies in the UK, so a great one to spot and to teach the kids. And of course they don't sting. Create a game and make the kids a little chart of real but fantastical creatures to find in the garden and offer a prize; it could be much more fun than playing Pokémon. (Ref 56).

Drone Fly (*Eristalis tenax*)

This hoverfly is very easily confused with honeybees; the Drone fly is a hoverfly that mimics the male honeybee, presumably to confuse predators. They are a similar size to honeybees and hang silently in the air in summer, often feeding on open daisy flowers. Look out for their large eyes that almost join in the middle. It's the one thing that flies can't change and a great way to tell bees and flies apart (bees have smaller eyes, on the sides of their heads). There are quite a few different species within the

It's easy to mistake the Drone fly (Eristalis tenax) for a male honeybee. © Martin Mulchinock.

Eristalis genus. Many hoverflies exhibit territorial behaviour (Ref 56) by guarding sunny spots where they 'hope' to find a mate.

One of them has really interesting courtship behaviour. The males of *Eristalis nemorum* hover above the females, sometimes in a stack of more than one or two, almost jockeying for position, though it could be part of the courtship dance.

The Drone fly adults feed on nectar and the larvae feed on rotting vegetation.

How to spot
Learn how to distinguish between bees and flies and you will quickly recognise the two-winged (Diptera), bug-eyed Drone flies. They are rather cute and regular visitors in the garden, often on flat flowers providing virtual dinner plates of nectar rich flowers in one place. If you think it's a honeybee take a good look at its eyes. The Drone fly mimics a honeybee perfectly but can't disguise its big fly eyes.

How to attract
Grow lots of open flowers in the garden, especially those in the daisy family, which have lots of central flower tubes filled with nectar. Leave a few containers of rainwater filled with rotting leaves and vegetation to mature and you will provide a perfect place for the adults to lay their eggs and exactly the right conditions for the larvae to feed and mature.

Hornet Mimic Hoverfly (*Volucella zonaria*)

Hoverflies are excellent bee mimics but this one takes it to the extreme and is a very realistic hornet mimic. When I first saw one I did a double take. I am not scared of hornets, but this is a very impressive insect and really does look like a hornet.

Take a close look at this pollinator. It is the Hornet Mimic hoverfly (Volucella zonaria) our largest UK hoverfly and a gentle giant. © Jean Vernon.

It's easy to see how it might deter a predator but it is another matter just how this handsome beast evolved. It is the largest hoverfly species in the UK, and more common in southern counties. Eighty years ago it was considered to be rare and has migrated here with the change in climate. Some years it is more common than others, thought to be enhanced by favourable weather conditions that support migration from Europe.

Adult Hornet Mimic hoverflies are found in southern counties of the UK. In some years populations may be topped up by migratory individuals from the continent (Ref 57) when the adults arrive in spring, lay their eggs, then the descendants leave in autumn. Its larvae live and feed on the nest debris inside the nests of social wasps. The insects share a symbiotic relationship; the larvae get a safe place to feed and mature and the wasps get a home help that keeps the nest neat and tidy.

How to spot
Look out for large golden yellow-banded insects in the garden. Hornets and hoverflies will feed on accessible nectar and though on first glance they do look similar, take a good look at the eyes. The Hornet Mimic has large chestnut brown eyes, quite a broad body and a yellow face.

How to attract
Start to notice the insects in your garden. Look more closely at what they are feeding on and try and identify which clan of mini beasts they belong too. Learn to live with wasps, as without their nests this species will not thrive. Start to see the beauty in the mini-beasts as well as the birds and the bees.

Bumblebee Hoverfly (*Volucella bombylans*)

These are cute and fluffy hoverflies that lay their eggs in the nests of bumblebees and some wasps. There are two main species that closely mimic different species of bumblebee and both are common. There's a white and yellow banded and a red tailed form and though you might think they would use their disguise to confuse bees with similar livery, research by Albert Ludwigs, Freiburg University (Ref 58), suggests otherwise. Complex scenarios involving different hoverfly females and bumblebee nests recorded no correlation between the appearance of the hoverfly and the nests it visited. The female needs to enter a nest and if she meets a bumblebee the researchers found she would be identified as an intruder and attacked. It concluded that she used the time between the in-and-out flights of the worker bees to enter the nest unnoticed. Inside, she digs herself into the nest and lays her eggs and if discovered, overwhelmed and stung, she is equipped with a mechanism that still allows her to lay her eggs quickly.

Some hoverflies are cute and fluffy! This is the Bumblebee hoverfly (Volucella bombylans) that looks like a bee but is really a fly. © Liam Olds

The hoverfly larvae feed on the nest debris and are thought to eat the host larvae too. Some volucella species are being used as a biological wasp control in New Zealand for social wasps. (Ref 59).

Narcissus Fly (*Merodon equestris*)

The Narcissus fly was the bane of the narcissus industry in years gone by. Daffodil bulbs are still heat-treated to control the larvae in commercially sold bulbs. It can still be a problem in gardens today where its larvae feed on the plump bulbs of daffodils and other fleshy bulbs of closely related genera (amaryllidacea), including snowdrops and nerines. But it does tend to affect damaged bulbs; and remember that the adults are hoverflies and important garden pollinators and a vital part of the garden ecosystem.

The Narcissus fly is a hoverfly that uses its stripy livery to deter predators. It usually lays its eggs around the base of daffodils or bluebells, which then hatch and feast on the fleshy bulbs.

ATTRACTING GARDEN POLLINATORS

Another bumblebee mimic, but this one lays its eggs around narcissi, earning it the enviable name of Narcissus fly.
© Liam Olds.

How to spot

The adult hoverflies look like mini bumblebees. They are fluffy or hairy, some are a fawn beige in colour, others are more golden and some are banded with white, black and brown hairs. Look out for them between mid-May and June when they will be searching for bulbs to lay their eggs.

How to attract

Leave a few sacrificial daffodils growing at the edge of the garden, maybe naturalised in the grass or on a bank. The adult flies prefer warm sheltered spots (Ref 60).

Plant more bulbs so that you can afford to lose some to these hoverfly larvae. Plant in clumps that are dispersed around the plot. Don't use pesticides. In the UK there are no approved garden chemicals that will work and it is better to encourage the natural balance in your garden and leave the wildlife to feast on larvae.

Marmalade Hoverfly (*Episyrphus balteatus*)

One of the most common hoverflies in the UK is affectionately known as the Marmalade hoverfly. It's a brightly coloured species with amber and black stripes, but stands out due to its rather cute moustache-like black bands on its abdomen. But it is the thick cut and thin cut stripes that give it its marmalade nickname.

It's a common visitor on garden flowers and a great one to get the kids to find as it doesn't sting, has funky markings and has huge bug eyes.

The adults lay their eggs near to colonies of aphids, so that when they hatch there is plenty of food for them to eat. This makes them fantastic 'pest' control for gardeners.

Some years huge numbers of this species arrive from Europe boosting the number feeding in gardens and the surrounding countryside.

Look out for the thin and thick cut Marmalade hoverfly, on bramble (rubus). © Jean Vernon.

How to spot
The Marmalade hoverfly is quite small, about 9–12mm long, and is on the wing all year round, though more common in the summer. Look out for the thick and thin black bands and the moustache shaped markings on the abdomen.

How to attract
Grow lots of flowers of all shapes and sizes. Avoid double flowers where the nectaries and pollen may be inaccessible or even bred out. Leave aphids for the larvae to feast on. Do some citizen science and join the Hoverfly Recording Scheme and help track these delicate creatures.

FUN HOVERFLY FACTS

Holy Hoverflies

Just when you think it couldn't get any more bizarre, one of our common hoverflies bears the Batman logo on its thorax. Affectionately known as the Batman hoverfly, look closely and you can see the distinctive shape. I can't think of a better way to get children out in the garden looking for Batman. Make it a treasure hunt, give them a camera and have a prize for the best picture of this insect hero.

Holy hoverfly, it's Batman. The Batman hoverfly (Myathropa florea) has the bat logo on its thorax. © Liam Olds.

The Jet Set

Researchers from the University of Exeter (Ref 61) studied the movement of migratory hoverflies and discovered that up to four billion migrate to and from Britain each year! That means these wanderlust creatures will pollinate billions and billions of flowers and produce offspring (larvae) that will munch their way through up to ten trillion aphids. Just as well they don't need a visa or vaccination certificate to visit. Yet!

Sweet Treat

Not all hoverflies feed from flowers. Some like the Xylota, Brachypalpoides and Chalcosyrphus feed on the sweet sticky honeydew, which is secreted by aphids. So instead of finding them on flowers you might see them running up and down the surface of leaves where they may also eat stray pollen grains (Ref 62).

Subterfuge

Many hoverflies mimic bees and wasps. This is called Batesian mimicry after the scientist Henry Walter Bates, who discovered it in the Victorian age. The bright stripy livery confuses predators and can give the hoverfly a few seconds to escape being eaten. Some take this a stage further and dangle their front legs so that they look like antennae, and others can actually pretend to sting by raising their abdomen in a similar action.

Sunbathing hoverflies (Syrphus spp) on cosmos deter predators with a stripy bee livery. © Jean Vernon.

The Buzz Effect

Hoverflies don't just mimic the look of bees, some can also replicate the sound of bumblebees, which could be a factor in deterring predators (Ref 62A).

Wings and Things

Hoverflies have an extra vein on their wings – one way to identify them from other insects. They also have two wings like all flies, rather than the four wings which bees and wasps have.

Pollen Rich

Wind pollinated plants such as grasses, plantains and sedges are all good hoverfly plants because they produce masses of pollen.

Early pollen bearing catkins are a perfect protein source for pollinators like this hoverfly (Eristalis pertinax).
© Jean Vernon.

Buzz Off

Some hoverflies show territorial behaviour and will chase off other insects to protect a mate.

Sticky Saliva

Hoverfly larvae, which predate on other insects are generally blind and locate their prey using chemical senses and touch. They have a pretty gruesome mode of action: they stick the prey to a surface with sticky saliva, pierce its skin and suck out the innards until just the husk remains (Ref 62).

Plant Miners

The plant feeding hoverfly larvae are less gruesome (unless you are a plant). Some feed on all parts of their host plants, from stems, leaves and roots. Others actually mine inside the stems, where they feed in safety and then chew an escape hatch so that they can pupate in the soil nearby (Ref 62).

Great for Kids

Hoverflies do not bite or sting and can be safely caught for identification and are great for engaging children. A butterfly net swept over the top of grassland and flowers should catch a few good samples.

Beneficial Creatures

Hoverfly adults don't live very long, but they are the gardener's friends, pollinating plants, devouring pests and keeping the natural balance.

Other flies

You could be forgiven for skipping this section, but don't. Flies repulse many people, but without them we would be in very serious trouble. Flies are actually the heroes of the garbage, the rubbish, the road kill and even death and decomposition. In fact flies and their larvae (maggots) have been used to unravel crime scene forensics; by studying the life stages of the eggs, larvae and adult species present it is possible to pinpoint the time of death. It's called forensic entomology and it works because flies are some of the first creatures attracted to a dead animal and quick to take advantage of the source of food for their offspring.

If you start to research flies, the first thing you find is article after article about how to get rid of them. And I'll be honest, I hate having flies around my kitchen in the summer – but I have started to see the beauty in them too.

With around 7,000 species of flies in the UK the diversity of this order of insects is extraordinary. From the minute midges that bite and bother us in the summer (but are also the creatures that pollinate the chocolate we love) to the detrivores and blow

The diptera family is very diverse and includes bee mimics and nature's recyclers. This is a Tachinid fly (Nowickia ferox) on aster. © Jean Vernon.

flies that devour the dead, to the fascinating bee flies. Like many invertebrate clades in nature, the flies are extremely varied and life is rarely cute and fluffy. While we should be hugely grateful to the role some flies play in the forensics of dead bodies and time of death, it's no surprise that flies don't usually feature very high on favourite pollinator lists. And yet many flies are pollinators too.

Flies are generally active in cooler temperatures than bees. They visit flowers for the energy rich nectar, which they use as a fuel for their activity, feeding from open flowers and bowl shaped flowers. Some will feed on pollen and others will lay their eggs in the flowers for their larvae to eat the seeds.

Most flies aren't as hairy or fluffy as bees, so they collect less pollen on their bodies, but they may be present in greater numbers and so still provide an effective pollination service for the plant.

Stinky Science

If you've a blue bottle in the house the chances are it's telling you that you've forgotten something that has now gone off. Flies are attracted to the smell of decomposition.

Some plants use this mechanism to effect pollination, by recreating such a stench that passing flies are attracted to what they think is rotting meat. It's another plant I 'met' at Royal Botanic Gardens Kew when I worked there during a summer vacation from university. A kindly botanist offered up a potted plant for me to smell the flower. One deep inhalation had me running for the door. For instead of a fragrant perfume, the offending plant, a stapelia with a beautiful frilly green bloom, emitted a stench of rotting flesh. I now know that this plant is known as the carrion plant. Blowflies are conned by the smell and lay their eggs on the flowers. When the larvae hatch they wriggle around and pollinate the flowers, but starve, as there is no meat to feed on. In the UK you might find yellow skunk cabbage (*Lysichiton americanus*) growing in bog gardens. Its musky skunk fragrance attracts pollinating flies and beetles in a similar way.

Flytraps

While not pollinators, it would be remiss not to mention the carnivorous plants that attract, trap and digest flies and other insects and even small mammals. Another of my gateway plants, the Venus Flytrap is a perfect plant to entrance and engage youngsters. The fascinating relationship between the plant and its insect prey is the stuff of nightmares and a magnet for plant-intrigued kids. Not only are the cartoonlike traps animated, you can trick the plant into closing by touching the trigger hairs inside the traps, mimicking a fly. The toothed trap keeps the fly in place as its digestive juices

ATTRACTING GARDEN POLLINATORS

Some plants have very intimate relationships with flies, like the Venus Flytrap (Dionaea muscipula).
© Martin Mulchinock.

dissolve the prey, absorbing the nutrients over a matter of days. I saved up my pocket money for weeks to buy a Venus Flytrap and then watched it like a hawk, waiting for it to score a fly for supper. Days went by and I worried it would starve so I fed it a scrap of corned beef and it died. I'm not sure what I learnt from that, but I was desperately disappointed. I still love seeing these plants at flower shows and when possible I can't help but activate the little traps, with permission of course!

Bee Fly (*Bombylius major* et al)

Look out for the Bee fly, a common spring garden pollinator that will feed on the nectar of primulas, aubrietia and pulmonaria. There are five species of these little flies that look like little flying shrews with proboscis extended. They also resemble bumblebees and flit very fast from flower to flower, supping nectar. Their fuzzy bodies will attract pollen and their keen visits to spring flowers aids pollination of several spring flowering plants.

This cute little Bee fly (Bombylius major) hides a dirty secret. Its eggs hatch out inside the nests of mining bees and wasps. © Gail Ashton.

Most female Bee flies collect little stones and soil dust into a cavity under their abdomen, and as they flick their sticky eggs out these are coated with the dust, making them heavier and probably more likely to reach into the nests of mining bees, where they hatch and devour the solitary bee larvae and developing bees (Ref 63).

The most common species of this fluffy fast flying fly is the Dark-edged Bee fly that has a brown band along the top of its wings, but there is a Dotted Bee fly that as its name suggests has beautifully spotted wings. These are more common in southern UK but are spreading northwards due to climate change. Often they are flying too fast to spot the difference.

There are nine species in the UK (Ref 64), although some are very uncommon. These flies are parasites of several solitary bee and wasp species, mostly the ground nesting mining bees and including the Ashy Mining bee.

How to spot

At first sight in spring you might think that this is a bumblebee feeding on spring flowers like aubrietia and primroses. The Bee fly has quite a loud buzz and a very prominent proboscis sticking out; some people call them Unicorn flies for this reason (Ref 65). It's a fast flier and quite difficult to capture in photographs. If you can count the wings there will be two (not four like a bee) and it has quite large eyes on the top of its head. They are usually active from February to June but most commonly seen in April. The timing of both the hosts and the parasite need to coincide for these flies to survive. Andrena, the mining bees, emerge and start laying their eggs around the same time as the Bee flies are on the wing.

How to attract

Bee fans might find it a little difficult thinking about how to help and support Bee flies, now that they know they parasitise the nests of mining bees. But without a healthy population of their hosts, the Bee flies cannot survive. The Bee fly has a long proboscis and needs spring flowers with corresponding tubular corollas and access to nectaries like the aubrietia, lungwort, primroses and anchusa.

Join in with the annual #BeeFlyWatch and log your Bee fly sightings to help scientists understand more about this creature.

Giant Tachinid Fly (*Tachina grosso*)

Stake out your nectar rich garden plants in summer and you might find these large parasitic flies feeding on the flowers. They resemble bumblebees in size and colouring and are actually hairy, which is unusual for flies. They lay their eggs onto other insect larva such as moth caterpillars, which are then eaten from

The bristly Tachinid fly (Tachina grosso) is a parasitic garden fly, and a pollinator feeding on majoram. © Jean Vernon.

the inside out. It's pretty gruesome, but yet another example of nature keeping control of every level of the food chain.

The Tachinid flies are important parasites of a variety of insects considered to be garden 'pests'. From a gardener's perspective these bristly flies help 'control' a variety of plant munching caterpillars and other leaf-eating insects. Whether you consider them to be friend or foe, Tachinid flies are an important part of our garden ecosystem and biodiversity.

There are many forms, some 270 species in the UK (Ref 66), which include the rather beautiful *Phasia hemiptera* which parastitises some of our garden shield bugs.

ATTRACTING GARDEN POLLINATORS

How to spot

Tachinid flies are very variable. They feed and meet to mate on nectar rich flowers such as wild marjoram where they may also linger and lurk until they spot their host species feeding. Look out for bristly looking insects on your flowers.

How to attract

Grow summer flowering, nectar rich flower species like marjoram. A healthy compost system may also attract and support these creatures. Live and let live, learn about new insects and their lifecycles, share with the children and stay in awe of nature and her complicated and intricate ways. Join the Tachinid recording scheme (Ref 67)and learn more about these flies.

Green Bottle (*Lucilia spp*)

Flies are incredibly variable. But even still I find most of them a little tricky to fall in love with. That was until I found a beautiful iridescent Green bottle feeding on my Dyer's chamomile. I was totally blown away by its beauty. And what a contrast to the pure, bright yellow daisy flowers. Wow.

An iridescent beauty, the Green bottle (Lucilia sericata) on Dyers chamomile (Anthemis tinctoria). © Jean Vernon.

But this beauty, like its close relative the Blue bottle lays its eggs in excrement and carcasses of creatures, where the larvae (maggots) feed on the decaying matter (Ref 68). If you find that disgusting, stop and consider that without this activity we would be knee deep in dead and decaying matter. They carry out a vital task, recycling and removing dead material and completing the cycle of death and rebirth.

How to spot
Green bottles are a stunning iridescent green colour. They can be found on garden flowers where they will nectar, wait for a mate or overnight in the garden. They seem to prefer stronger smelling flowers like mint, alliums, and cabbages and are considered to be important pollinators.

How to attract
Make a compost heap to support the different stages of decomposition in your garden. Plant pongy plants and allow them to flower. Learn a little bit more about some of your garden visitors and try to see the beauty in everything you see and find. Each and every creature has a part to play in your garden.

Owl Midge (*Psychodidae spp*)

These little fluffy flies look a bit like a cross between a barn owl and a moth, shrunk into Alice's wonderland. When you know they are also called drain flies, filter flies, moth flies and sewage flies, you start to understand a little more about their lifecycle. They are about 90 species in the UK and they are almost impossible to identify, at least by amateurs. But just like the Chocolate midge that pollinates our precious cocoa plants, the Owl midge is a pollinator too. The adult females are attracted to the pongy inflorescence of the cuckoo pint also known as lords and ladies and wild arum among other common names (Ref 69). The flowers emit a decaying scent (Ref 70) and have a unique way of offering a warm and safe place by raising the internal temperature of the flower. The Owl midges arrive *en masse* looking for somewhere to lay their eggs and become trapped by the hairs at the base of the flower (Ref 71).

The arum needs cross pollination to set seed. If the midges have come from another plant and bear pollen, then by crawling around in the bottom of the flower they transfer the pollen to the stigmas and effect pollination. Otherwise they pick up pollen that falls from the anthers from this flower while trapped, and when the hairs wither, the owl flies move on taking the pollen with them.

Is it an owl or a moth? No, it's an Owl midge (Psychodidae spp). © Brian Gort Wildlife.

How to spot

If you've got cuckoo pint growing near you it's worth having a look at the flowers when they emerge to see if you can spot the little Owl midges. But the plants are poisonous and the midges are small.

How to attract

It's unclear whether the Owl midge needs the arum to complete its lifecycle, but the arum needs the midge. The best way to help maintain and support these unique relationships is to regard your garden as a complex and amazing ecosystem and work with nature to keep it healthy. Feed the soil rather than the plants. Embrace a little decay and decomposition. Stop using garden chemicals and let the predator/prey balance restore. Garden for wildlife and let nature be the judge and the jury when it comes to perceived problems.

St Mark's Fly (*Bibio marci*)

The St Mark's flies are so named because they first emerge in April around St Mark's Day (25 April) but they are also on the wing all summer and there are 20 different species of them.

These St Mark's flies are head down supping nectar from a thistle flower. © Jean Vernon.

Also known as bibionid flies and hawthorn flies, their larvae might be found in little clusters in the lawn. The dark grey-brown grubs are legless and feed on organic material and decaying matter. They are excellent detrivores, tidying up rotting leaves and thatch within the matrix of the grass roots. They are also a great source of natural food for songbirds and ground feeders.

The adult flies feed on nectar on a variety of flowers and are important pollinators of fruit trees (Ref 72). They are often present in large numbers and are sluggish feeders, staying in one place for a long time. This makes them good pollinators (Ref 73).

St Mark's flies don't live very long as an adult, around a week. But the males often fly sluggishly in groups, hovering in the air and flying at head height, with their legs dangling down. They are cruising around seeking out females, hoping to attract a mate.

That makes them quite conspicuous and easy to spot if you are out and about in spring, especially near woodland, hedgerows and along riverbanks. The males are smaller and their eyes do not join at the top and are divided by a groove. Each eye has a separate connection to its brain. This allows male bibionid flies to do more than one thing at a time! The upper eye part is used to look for females, while the lower part can monitor the fly's position relative to the ground, which enables them to hover in one place (Ref 74).

The females have smaller heads and eyes, smoky brown wings and often have red tinged legs (think funky red/orange stockings so that you remember which is which).

  ATTRACTING GARDEN POLLINATORS

How to spot

These little black flies are about 12–14mm long and thin. They have large eyes and long dangling legs (Ref 75).

Look out for them nectaring on flowers. These flies do not bite or sting and are completely harmless. They are important garden pollinators that should be revered and not feared.

How to attract

Hold off the lawn treatments. Leave part of your garden a little bit wild and unkempt. Don't cut everything down neat and tidy, leave a bit of leaf mould, use a composter and learn to appreciate every part of the food chain.

FLY FLOWERS

If you really wanted to grow a plant that was just perfect for flies then dipterists would say grow hogweed (Ref 76). But the trouble with hogweed is that it is a thug and its leaves and sap can be an irritant, sometimes with extreme effects. However, many of the umbellifers (now correctly called apiaceae) are good fly plants, and of course flies include hoverflies too.

Apiaceae are also known as the carrot family, which includes other great garden plants like lovage, fennel, angelica and Queen Anne's lace. Carrots are biennial and flower in their second year of growth, but you can grow carrot plants from the tops cut off your carrots. Root them in compost and let them flower to feed the pollinators; it's a great project for the kids.

The flower heads of umbellifers/apiaceae will support a wide range of delicate flies. © Jean Vernon.

Beetles

Beetles are not the most obvious pollinators in our gardens. But some of them are surprising pollinators existing before many of the more familiar pollinators walked on and flew around our planet.

Some of the most stunning trees adorning botanical gardens and arboretums across the nation are beetle pollinated. Magnolias evolved somewhere around 95 million years ago, long before there were bees, butterflies and moths. The beetles, searching for protein rich pollen, were drawn to the large, flamboyant magnolia flowers.

The flowers cleverly offer first mature pollen-rich male parts that are clumsily chewed by the beetles. The later maturing female flower parts look similar and as the beetles examine and chew flower parts in search of pollen they transfer pollen from younger flowers. It's all a bit clumsy and thought to be why magnolia petals and sepals are tough and leathery. Beetles are sometimes called the dumb pollinators, but considering that they worked out they could find pollen to eat within flowers long before our friends the bees appeared on the scene, that seems harsh. Flower visiting beetles may in fact be better pollinators in places with fewer bees (Ref 77).

Growing up in south east London I didn't realise what a privilege it was to see and have Stag Horn beetles living in the woods around our school. But I remember these huge beetles taking centre stage in a school assembly presentation and learning about

Beetles are vital detrivores laying their eggs in fallen timber. A few are pollinators, but others like the Stag Horn beetle are gateway insects, teaching young and old about these incredible creatures. © Gail Ashton.

Back a few million years early plants like magnolias were pollinated by beetles feeding on pollen. © Jean Vernon.

their incredible fiery fights and flights in midsummer when the heavily horned males duel over the females.

Incredibly the larvae live and feed on rotting tree stumps, also a rare commodity in today's health and safety tidied woodlands, for four to six years.

Thick-Legged Flower Beetle (*Oedemera nobilis*)

What an aptly named little creature, though it is also called the false oil beetle (Ref 78). The Thick-legged beetle is probably the first beetle I ever noticed inside a flower. I was struck by its iridescent jewel-like wings, its huge fat thighs and its long, quirky antennae. And although I was first told it was the females that had fat legs, which I thought was a bit sexist, it turns out it is the males. The large swollen femora are a distinctive feature of this common garden beetle that frequents gardens and meadows in the southern half of the UK. These pollen feeders move from flower to flower and frequent poppies, ox eye daisies, roses, cornflowers, brambles and daisies,

Pollen feeding beetles like the Fat-legged beetle (Oedemera nobilis). © Jean Vernon.

where they act as efficient pollinators. The larvae develop inside hollow dry stems where they feed and grow before emerging as adults.

How to spot
Look out for these iridescent beetles in summer flowers on warm days. It's easier to spot the fat legged males than the females, though both may be present. Take photographs to make a positive identification.

How to attract
Grow more of the plants that these beetles like. That means poppies, brambles and daisies. Plant in clumps and give them space to establish so that they provide many flowers over several weeks. Choose organic plants or grow from seed to be sure that they have not been treated with pesticides during their growth.

Pollen Beetles (*Meligethes aeneus*)

If you live near yellow fields of rapeseed, or you grow lots of garden flowers, you've probably noticed these little green or black beetles inside your flowers. Pollen beetles eat pollen and can be found on garden flowers from spring, when they emerge from winter and start to feed. You might find them on daffodils, and they seem to have a preference for yellow, but will also feed on the pollen inside roses, sweet peas and other garden flowers. The adult females lay their eggs on flower buds of brassicas; the larvae feed inside the flowers and then pupate in the soil. The adults emerge in late summer

Friend or foe? These pollen munchers, the Pollen beetles (Meligethes aeneus), *are pollinators too. © Jean Vernon.*

and overwinter to repeat the cycle. Pollen beetles don't damage garden plants but they can be a problem in cut flowers or where they are present in huge numbers. Nevertheless they have a role to play; they are pollinators and should not be controlled. Spraying open flowers with pesticides can have drastic effects on pollinating insects of all types. Avoid using garden pesticides to allow the natural balance to restore.

If you bring flowers indoors that have pollen beetles inside, put them in a vase in a cool shed or dark room and place them near the window for a few hours, the beetles will fly out towards the light leaving your flowers beetle-free.

How to spot
Look out for the little 2–3mm black or green beetles inside your garden flowers. They are especially common when the rapeseed is in flower. You might also find them on other yellow flowers.

How to attract
Plant pollen rich plants all around your garden choosing varieties that flower in succession, so that all garden pollinators have a suitable source of pollen and nectar.

Common Red Soldier Beetle (*Rhagonycha fulva*)

Once you start looking at the insects in your garden you are going to come across this little beauty. It has a few names, one of which describes a common summer pose – the bonking beetle – because you often find them mating in your summer garden. Apparently they spend most of their short lives mating. And sometimes there are lots of them. And once you recognise them you will smile every time you see them. It's a good thing for gardeners that there are lots of these around because the adults feed on garden aphids and the larvae eat all sorts of ground dwellers like slugs and snails.

Look out for common Soldier beetles (Rhagonycha fulva) en masse on your garden flowers. They are not called bonking beetles without good reason. © Gail Ashton.

But the adults also eat pollen and nectar and this means they are common inside the flowers and active garden pollinators. They are quite cute too with long wavy antennae and a red/orange overcoat.

How to spot
Look out for these orange, red and black beetles in your gardens. They like umbellifers and also daisies and are important pollinators for hogweed and cow parsley.

How to attract
Plant a few more umbellifers (apiaceae) in your garden. Things like wild carrot, fennel, angelica, lovage and cow parsley. Add some asters and other daisy flowers like echinacea and rudbeckia; even if the soldier beetles don't like them they will be good for other garden pollinators.

Ladybirds (*Coccinellidae spp*)

You might be surprised to learn that one of the gardener's best friends, the ladybird, is also a pollinator. Ladybirds are common garden beetles, which feed mostly on aphids, but also top up their energy levels with flower nectar, and though they are more interested in protein-rich prey they can and will eat pollen from flowers too. The red-coated, spotty adult Ladybirds fly from plant to plant looking for food and as they do this they pick up pollen on their bodies, which can be transferred to other flowers. It doesn't make them great pollinators, but the fact that they can

The iconic garden Ladybird is predator and pollinator rolled into one. © Martin Mulchinock.

transfer pollen from flower to flower does facilitate pollination where that pollen is compatible to the recipient flower stigma.

It's a great example of how nature provides. Ladybirds have evolved so that their lifecycle coincides with the creatures they eat. Just as the aphid populations start to establish in the garden, the Ladybirds emerge from hibernation to feast on these green sapsuckers. The adults feed and mate and then the females lay their precious eggs on stinging nettles and the cycle starts again.

Gardeners revere Ladybirds due to their voracious appetite for aphids, but they also eat a wide variety of other grubs and insects that might attack your garden plants. Rather than soaking your plants with toxic pesticides to destroy perceived garden 'pests' it is far more effective to support and encourage the natural balance, including Ladybirds.

How to spot

You can't fail to recognise the red-coated Ladybird, though there are about 46 different species that may frequent your UK garden and these are very varied in their colouring, markings and appearance. And don't forget the Ladybird larvae, which are very unusual in appearance.

It's a great reminder that not everything in the garden is a pest. Ladybird larvae look pretty weird, but each one eats a massive amount of aphids and other plant 'pests' before it pupates into an adult beetle.

Not all garden friends are pretty. Ladybird larvae look like fierce mini dinosaurs but are voracious aphid feeders.
© Martin Mulchinock.

How to attract

Plant plants with pollen rich flowers. Leave the aphids for the predators and plant things that aphids love too. Without a decent population of 'food' ladybirds will move elsewhere to feast. So if your garden is sterile and you spray every time you see a 'pest' not only will you destroy the food of many beneficial insects, but you risk killing the very creatures you want to support. Insecticides are not selective; that means they will kill most insects whether or not you consider them to be good or bad.

Think about overwintering sites. Ladybirds often hunker down in seed heads, plant crowns and hollow stems. In my garden many overwinter in the sedum roof on my garden shed. And remember to leave a clump of nettles in a sunny spot in the garden for them to lay their eggs on.

Wasp Beetle (*Clytus arietis*)

One of nature's mimics, the Wasp beetle looks like a wasp but is a type of longhorn beetle (Ref 79). Like many wasp mimics its vibrant livery gives it a head start when a predator approaches. Its yellow stripy carapace features contrasting yellow stripes on black hinting that it might not be so good to eat. It's a woodland, hedgerow species but if you live in the countryside you might find it in your garden. The adult lays her eggs in dry dead wood of willow and birch where the larvae mature. The adults are excellent pollinators feeding in hedgerow flowers from May to July. It's widespread in England and Wales but scarcer in Scotland.

Just when you thought you'd seen everything, here is a beetle that looks like a wasp. © Liam Olds.

CHAPTER THREE

Important Pollinator Habitats

Your garden is a nature reserve. Whatever size it is, it provides a variety of habitats for wildlife. We can all add to our gardens, or indeed design a border or a complete garden for pollinators. Even a tiny balcony or patio garden offers nesting, resting, breeding and feeding sites for a range of creatures. If we linked up all the gardens together they would form 270,000 hectares (Ref 80) of vital sanctuary for a range of wildlife and especially our garden pollinators. And that's because within and around our gardens is a huge diversity of habitat that these precious creatures need. Let me explain.

Ponds

Water is essential for life and by adding a pond or a bog garden to your plot you are creating a fantastic wildlife habitat that will also be of huge benefit to pollinators too. Some of our common pollinators like the hoverfly Drone flies have aquatic larvae. You can create small hoverfly lagoons for these creatures, but a pond is even better, especially with a shallow edge and some decaying timber and leaves. Pond

Every wildlife garden needs a pond. It's an essential garden habitat. © Jean Vernon.

plants can be good for many pollinators and add a whole new dimension to your planting, introducing bog plants and water plants to your palette of plants. A muddy edge provides building materials for mason bees (and even nesting birds), which use mud to seal their egg cells. Create a stepped edge to the pond to allow wildlife to enter and leave safely but also to provide for the different species of mini beasts that are found at different stages between the aquatic and terrestrial environment.

Flowering Plants

You might be surprised to see flowers on the list of garden habitats, but some flowers provide shelter for all sorts of pollinators during their precarious life cycle. In particular, when bumblebees emerge in early spring, they spend some time searching for an appropriate nesting site. Imagine that they emerge on a sunny day in early spring, the warmth of the sun brushing their winter shelter, warming their bodies and heralding the coming of spring. They need to find food quickly to fuel their activities and in February and March there's a dearth of garden flowers. If they are lucky, and remember they won't fly great distances, there will be some crocus, hellebores and snowdrops flowering in your garden. They need the nectar to give them energy and they will be virtually starving after months of torpor (Ref 81), often underground. The short days and the brief sunny spells can make nest searching tough. So if you find a huge fluffy bumblebee inside crocus flowers in the garden, there's a good chance that it has spent the night sheltering inside the flower. Don't forget, if you find a struggling bumblebee in early spring it is more than likely a queen. She may need to warm up in the sunshine, or perhaps you can carefully move her to a nectar rich flower to feed and regain her composure.

As the season progresses and the male bumblebees hatch and emerge, they are out in your garden *en masse*. Once the males

Many insects shelter inside flowers. Here a posse of beetles seeks refuge inside a carrot flower. © Jean Vernon.

ATTRACTING GARDEN POLLINATORS

leave the nest they are not allowed back in and they have to find food and shelter to survive. In summer you can find male bees (they are pretty much only around in summer and early autumn) inside flowers in the early morning, sometimes several in the same flower. So your actual garden flowers can provide an overnight stop, virtually a floral bed and breakfast for bees. How amazing is that? And it's not just bees that use flowers as shelter; some beetles for instance might shelter inside a carrot flower cluster, using its dense protected form as a buffer against rain and cold.

Bare Soil

Gardeners often strive to fill every gap in the border with more plants, but spare a thought for the ground nesters like the mining bees and the moth larvae that develop in the soil. Every time you dig in the borders you are destroying vital habitat. Try and leave an area in the veg garden or the flower border undisturbed so that invertebrates can shelter, nest or breed there. Even bare patches or closely mown areas in the lawn can be essential habitat for different species of digger wasps, mining bees and pupating moths.

Flowerpots and Planters

Apart from the plants that you grow in garden containers, providing a virtual fast food diner for pollinators, sometimes your pots and planters are chosen by all sorts of pollinators to overwinter and nest in too. Leaf-cutter bees like nesting in flowerpots, building little cigar like cocoons under the compost.

Queen wasps, queen bumblebees and even moth pupa may be buried under the surface, especially when they are in a sheltered spot, a greenhouse or a garden shed. It's rare but it does happen and gardeners need to be aware. A container of plants full of crumbly compost can be the perfect spot, especially when they are brought in to shelter for the duration of winter. Take care when you remove the summer plants from your planters. Be gentle when you plant spring

*If you've ever found little stubby cigar-like packets, made from leaf segments, in a flowerpot, safe inside are Leaf-cutter bees.
© Brigit Strawbridge Howard.*

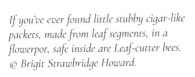

flowering bulbs into your pots and containers. Be aware that there may be a pollinator or even a queen bumblebee or wasp sheltering within the compost and if you accidently uncover them, try to put them back where you found them, or place them into a flower pot of leaves in a sheltered spot nearby.

Tussocky Grass

If you've only got a small garden you probably won't have any tussocky grass, but it's good to be aware of the type of habitat that some pollinators use and need. Grass tussocks are common in some grassland areas that may adjoin or be near your garden. If so you are lucky because tussocky grass is one of the requirements of some of the rarest bumblebees, as well as a wide variety of butterfly and moth caterpillars, which feed and pupate around grassy mounds.

The carder bees, particularly the Common Carder bee, the Moss Carder bee, the Brown-banded Carder bee and the very rare Shrill Carder bee, use the dead grass and moss as insulation for their nests. They don't generally nest in these grassy towers, preferring to make shallow surface nests that are warmed by the sun, but other pollinators can and do. Leave a patch of grass in your garden to grow wild. Don't sweep up all the leaves or tidy up the moss, these materials are nest liners for all sorts of pollinators, birds and other creatures too.

Remember that there are ornamental grass species that you could choose to grow that once established may themselves provide the right conditions for nesting and overwintering pollinators. Pampas grass is enjoying a bit of a revival and its clump forming roots can create a woody airy environment for rodents, beetles and bumblebees. On a smaller scale clumps of rusty coloured Carex planted on a slope may also create just the right conditions.

Dry Stone Walls

If you wanted to add a really valuable habitat to your garden, then see if you can make a dry stone wall somewhere. It could be a sculptural pile of rocks, or even a garden seat, but a dry stone wall makes a great nesting habitat for bumblebees and wasps and sometimes solitary bees too. It's a safe place for reptiles like the common lizard and slow worms. Dry stone walls look great too.

If you have an old wall and it's not a structural part of a building, then don't repoint it; leave it to weather for the wildlife. Mason bees might nest in the mortar, so keep a look out and don't disturb them or interfere with their nests. They are a true blessing and something to be nurtured and treasured.

Old rodent holes, drystone walls, cracks and crevices are all nesting sites for pollinators. In early spring queen bumblebees will be searching for a safe place to nest. © Jean Vernon.

Mossy Banks

If you have north facing bank of soil in the garden it may also be mossy. Moss thrives in damp shade and in low nutrient levels. The soil in a bank is raised above the ground and is actually a favourite place for queen bumblebees to overwinter if it faces north. That way it stays mostly in the shade over winter and the resting beauty isn't warmed up when the sun shines, so she isn't lured out of her winter torpor too early.

Other mossy garden banks and soil mounds may first attract the attention of small rodents like mice and voles, and when they vacate a nest these are often taken over by new queen bumblebees, who will use the ready excavated cavity to build a nest. Queen wasps may also overwinter under a blanket of moss. And of course a well-drained sandy bank is the perfect nesting site for many solitary bees and wasps. A few of the carder bees, especially the Moss Carder bee, the Common Carder bee and the Brown-banded Carder bee make shallow nests using moss to insulate them, and a mossy bank in a sunnier spot may well attract these bumblebee species.

Leave the moss to grow wherever you can. Far from being a pest, it is a beautiful plant in its own right and has many uses for wildlife, from lining birds' nests, to insulating homes.

Greenhouse

A garden greenhouse is rarely the choice for nest building but occasionally you may find overwintering queen bees and even queen wasps inside a flowerpot in a cold greenhouse. These will emerge earlier than they might if they had overwintered buried in the garden soil, but they will have spent the winter in a dry and protected place. More likely you will find queen bumblebees and other pollinators stuck inside your glasshouse in spring, especially if early spring flowers lure them there. Automatic greenhouse vents are notorious for allowing the pollinators to access the plants when the sun is shining, but trapping them in the greenhouse as the temperature drops. Check daily for trapped insects. Arm yourself with a spider vacuum to reach corners and gently remove them from the glasshouse eaves, placing them on nectar-rich flowers so that they can feed and return to their nest.

Once it becomes an established part of your garden environment you may start to find some pollinators breeding in your greenhouse. I often find overwintered Ladybirds and hoverfly larvae on my greenhouse plants, which is great because I know they will help to keep the aphids under control.

Compost Bin

Just like a raised bank of soil, a garden compost heap can be the perfect place for many garden pollinators to overwinter, shelter, breed and nest. Beetles, wasps and bees might make a nest within its protected walls. Many gardeners will only realise that their compost bin is now home to a colony of bees or wasps just when they start to garden in earnest in spring. While you can move a bumblebee nest it really is best to leave it alone. And I definitely wouldn't recommend moving a wasp nest. Moving or disturbing a nest constitutes an attack on the colony and you are likely to be stung. Having a bumblebee or wasp nest anywhere in your garden is a real privilege. And just as important, these pollinators will forage in and around your garden effecting pollination of your flowers, fruit and vegetables and adding their fabulous dimension of sound to the borders. The wasps will keep insect pests at bay. Your compost will continue to rot down beautifully with the nest still there and will be all the better for your garden with the extra composting time. You can start a new compost heap or bin somewhere else so that you can add your garden and kitchen waste to that rather than disturbing your newly acquired garden friends. The bees or wasps will benefit from the warmth of the composting material and if they are inside a compost bin they will have added protection from the wind and the rain.

Keep a close eye on them but don't disturb them; they are fascinating to watch and the kids will love learning about them too. As spring fades to summer the colony will start to produce adult males that are banished from the nest and can be found around the garden. They can't sting. Then the new season virgin queens will emerge and find a mate and then the old nest will die out. Once the nest has become inactive you can excavate it from the compost bin.

It's fascinating to have a look inside a nest. Bumblebee nests have little Winnie the Pooh nectar pots inside and wasps make a papier mâché citadel. You can then remove the compost and use it as a soil conditioner over the autumn and winter, emptying your compost bin, ready to start filling it again in spring.

Bird Box

An old used bird box is often adopted by some of the recent additions to the UK's bumblebee species. Commonly referred to as the Tree bumblebees, these bees like to nest up high and an old Blue Tit box is just about the right size and in a good place for a Tree bumblebee nest. You might also find them nesting under the eaves of your house. Wherever they choose they won't be there all year. Like all the bumblebees they start building their colonies in spring and by late summer/ early autumn the work is done and the new generation of young queens have been produced ready to overwinter and start their own colony next year.

Beware. Of all the bumblebees these are possibly the feistiest. While it might be possible to block up the nest box hole and move a contained nest, it really is better to leave the bees alone and enjoy watching them instead. One of the most exciting and fascinating things you might be lucky enough to see is when the male bees emerge in summer: they hang around *en masse* outside the bird box waiting for the new queen bees to emerge.

At the end of summer, when the colony has died out, you can clean out the bee nest and ready your bird box for spring. Put it somewhere where a bumblebee colony won't bother you, and then wait and see whether the Blue Tits or another Tree bumblebee queen will take it over. Bumblebees have been known to oust nesting tits from a bird box. So make sure you install plenty of nest boxes for both if your garden is a popular nest site.

Lawn

The lawn, that green grassy area in the middle of your garden, could be pollinator heaven. But you need to rethink your lawn care regime. If you've got a big lawn, fantastic, leaving part of it to grow wildflowers would help your garden pollinators immensely. Or you could simply raise the cutting height of your mower and let the lawn bloom. Many plants regarded as lawn weeds are forced to grow flat against the turf by the continual pruning of the mower blades. It is these plants such as self heal, clover, bird's foot trefoil, daisies and buttercups that will flower and feed your garden pollinators if you let the grass grow a little longer.

By mowing the grass up until late May or early June and then letting the lawn flora flower you can provide flowers to fill the 'June gap' in floral resources and extra food for your garden pollinators. Many grasses are larval plants for butterflies and moths.

But your lawn area is much more than a source of food; take a close look at the bare soil in your lawn. Just as important is actually keeping an area of lawn closely mown and sparsely grassed. If you've got little piles of soil between the grass plants that look like mini volcanoes, then you've got mining bees or digger wasps nesting in your lawn.

Wow. These are solitary creatures, but sometimes they nest together, so although each nest is independent and self sufficient, you can and do find a lot of them in one place. If your soil is well drained and sandy, mining bees in particular will just love it. Look a little closer and you will see the busy females, single mums attending the nest and bringing back food for their offspring to feed on when they hatch out as larvae. Keep your mower away from these areas while nesting activity is obvious, mow after dusk if you must. Instead, enjoy the spectacle of these little insects tooing and froing with provisions for their nests.

Hedges

If you have boundaries around your garden where a mixed hedge could replace a fence, this it is a great way to support the garden wildlife. Hedges are really important habitats for all sorts of creatures, from the larger and appropriately named hedgehogs, to the birds, and right down to the beetles and other pollinators. Nectar feeders will feed on the flowers of the hedge plants and in early spring some of the wild hedges are essential food sources for these creatures and especially emerging queen bees. Blackthorn, hawthorn, crab apple, elder, hazel and willow are important early food sources for pollinators. But there's an often overlooked early spring blossom that bridges winter into spring, the cherry plum (Ref 82), which has early blossom and edible fruit too. Once the flowers have been pollinated and set seed and fruit, this becomes food for birds and other animals. But under and around the base of the hedge is also an important habitat. Letting the leaves build up a little improves the biodiversity of the garden, attracting beetles and other mini beasts, but it is also a popular place for bumblebee nests and also for overwintering queens.

Alternate your hedge trimming so that your hedges can flower and mature. If at all possible cut every three to four years, by cutting just a section each year on a four-year rotation, so that it can mature and flower and provide a varied habitat for different wildlife and vital food for caterpillars of butterflies and moths.

Vertical Surfaces

Don't forget to make the most of any walls, trellises, fences and screens in and around the garden. You can train flowering climbers up a trellis or wires on a garden wall and provide additional forage for your local pollinators.

Fix a special bracket to the wall and hang a basket full of seasonal flowering plants. It will look amazing and provide extra food plants and help attract garden pollinators. But remember, no pesticides, and make sure you buy plants that have not been pretreated with systemic insecticides.

Wood/Timber

In nature wood is broken down by microbes and fungi that cause it to decay. Garden timber that has been treated against rot is saturated in chemicals and not suitable for nesting insects. But natural untreated timber, such as fallen branches and old tree stumps, are quickly colonised by all manner of mini beasts that make holes and crevices in them. Tiny woodworm holes and larger woodpecker holes are all perfect nest sites for cavity nesting bees. Some beetles like the Longhorn beetles nest and feed in rotting wood and some hoverfly species will use wet tree hollows thick with rotting leaves to lay their eggs.

Fallen branches, dead decaying timber and even a pile of logs can become home to wood boring insects and cavity nesters. © Jean Vernon.

Collect your garden prunings and make a log pile. It's a safe place for creatures to overwinter or hibernate. Every piece of natural deadwood can be used to support the balance in your garden. Place piles in different areas of the garden, from full sun to deep shade, to cater for different needs.

Drill holes into dead wood to attract cavity nesting bees and wasps. Leave deadwood in ponds and at pond margins for aquatic hoverflies and other creatures to use and to allow fungi to work on the timber. Most invertebrates are dependent on the action of fungi feeding on or within dead wood, which makes it an important habitat for everything from microbes to mini beasts.

Old trees and hollow trees are a rare commodity, but if you have a mature garden tree leave it be. It could be the perfect home for the saproxylic pollinators that are dependent on dead and decaying wood.

Stems and Plants

Tidy gardens can be a desert for some wildlife. It's all very well having lovely nectar rich flowers for insects, but you need to ensure that there are safe places for nesting sites and places to overwinter undisturbed. Some hollow stems, especially those that have been pre bored by beetles are the perfect overwintering sites for all sorts of creatures from bees to caterpillars and even beetles and ladybirds. Thick bramble stems are also used in this way.

Cutting down all the border stems and spent flowers in autumn can deprive precious creatures of the perfect place to overwinter. Some will bury themselves into the friable soil around the base of your plants while others may even nest in hollow stems of some of your plants. But other pollinators need additional resources, like the Wool Carder bee which uses the hairs of hairy plants to make her nest, or the leaf-cutter bees that need suitable leaves to carve into pieces to line their egg cells. Think twice before you add your garden stems to the bonfire or in to the shredder; something precious may be nesting there. Instead, leave the seed heads and decaying stems in place. The birds will devour any seeds they can access and the crispy spent stems and last year's growth will help insulate anything below. When you do decide it's time to tidy up, be careful where you poke your pruners. Leave the cut stems in a pile somewhere undisturbed to allow creatures to emerge safely in spring, and leave as much material *in situ* as you can.

Insect Houses

You can create additional habitats for many garden pollinators by making or buying a special insect house. When designed for insects and not as a piece of garden sculpture, these can and do attract a range of garden pollinators looking for suitable

Design an insect house to suit your needs. A block of wood bored with different diameter holes, sheltered inside a dry casing, is ideal for cavity nesters. © Martin Mulchinock/Marc Carlton.

nesting sites, such as mason bees and leaf-cutter bees. There are dozens of different designs and you can of course make your own.

When it comes to insect 'hotels', it's important to understand that the guests spend many months inside these boxes, starting off as eggs and maturing into larvae and finally adults, so they are more than a weekend retreat or a temporary home.

Unmanaged 'bug hotels' can provide nesting sites for all manner of other garden creatures and mini beasts. In a large garden designed for wildlife that may be perfectly OK, but if your intent is to have a house for solitary bees then you need to do a bit more than just give it space in your garden.

Whatever you do follow a few rules.

- It's essential that the creatures inside these insect houses, bee or bug boxes do not get wet or damp. They can usually withstand the cold but not the wet. Choose a design that is waterproof and be ready to move your chosen nest box into a cold but protected shed for the worst of the winter.
- The insect box needs to face south for the best results, so that it gets the best of the season's sun.
- Most designs need to be positioned 2–3 feet above ground.
- Hollow nesting tubes should have a closed end at the back; open-ended tubes are not suitable.
- Natural materials are the best. Don't use plastic, which will create condensation and encourage fungal problems.
- Choose an insect house that can be opened up for cleaning.
- Protect the face of your insect box with chicken wire to prevent predators feasting on the developing larvae.
- Don't neglect your insect box from year to year. It needs to be managed to ensure that the developing larvae survive and thrive.

Most insect house designs will attract a few species of garden bees to nest but it's important to understand that with these bees also come the parasites and predators that prey upon them. This is where it gets a bit scary because it's a bit like a version of *Alien* (Ref 83). But it's also important to note that this is nature, bug eat bug happens and everything has a place in nature, the food chain and a healthy rich garden biodiversity, even those that we perceive to be the baddies. Some of which, like the parasitic wasps, are pollinators themselves.

While the presence of these 'pests' is an indication of a healthy population of the host upon which they depend, let's be honest, most people that put an insect house in the garden are doing that to help garden pollinators. If that's your intention, but you don't want to manage or maintain your insect house then save your money and buy a bird or bat box instead.

If however you want to engage the children in the wonderful world of the pollinators and solitary bees then invest in a specially designed insect house that can be opened and cleaned, and offers an observation window into the world of the developing bee. It might cost more than you planned to spend, but it can be managed and reused for many years.

The award winning Nurturing Nature Solitary Observation Nest Box (Ref 84) is an excellent design. Made from timber it's inspired by nature and driven by science. Wildlife World makes interactive insect houses from FSC certified timber.

The whole point of these is that at the end of the season in about October you can very gently excavate the cocoons inside the nesting tubes and gently clean them, removing any which have been damaged or attacked. Those that are perfect can be safely kept in a special overwintering box, with ventilation somewhere cool and dry until the adults start to emerge in spring. It's a fantastic way to learn more about solitary bees and a great way to engage the children.

Snail Shells

Yes I am serious. Just when you thought that the snails in your garden were nothing but a pesky pest, I'm going to tell you a bit more about the vital role they play in the greater good of the garden. Snails are fantastic creatures, feeding on the dead and decaying matter in the garden as well as a few choice shoots of your favourite plants. Plants are the base layer of the food chain and support the layers above. Snails are also a great food source for many creatures, especially our beloved song thrushes, so rarely seen in our gardens. The spent shells of snails are a vital source of calcium to nesting birds, but there's another very rare creature that uses snail shells in a most remarkable way. The Snail Nester bee actually uses old, empty snail shells to make her nests. It's a perfect, waterproof home for her developing eggs and the mother bee moves an empty shell until it is in just the right position for her to make a nest.

Bee enthusiast/expert Brigit Strawbridge Howard calls these bees pesto bees, which sums up exactly how they seal their egg chambers, with masticated vegetable material

ATTRACTING GARDEN POLLINATORS

Look closer at this snail shell. It's been bunged up with masticated leaves by the Snail nester bee (Osmia bicolor).
© Jean Vernon.

stuffed into the shell entrance. It's not a common species and you'd be very privileged to find them on your plot, but it could happen and just being aware of the existence of these bees goes some way to spreading the word and the love about pollinators. So next time you find a snail shell in the garden, take a close careful look to see if it's been bunged up with garden pesto. If it has rejoice in the knowledge that your garden has been chosen by the delightful Snail Nester bees. It puts a whole new slant on garden snails and I hope makes you look more kindly on these little creatures. Remember Brian the *Magic Roundabout* snail? I'll leave you to think about that.

CHAPTER FOUR

Plants for Pollinators

If you take a look on the Internet for good plants for pollinators you will find dozens of plant lists. But when you don't know your plants or want more information these lists can be incredibly frustrating. Plant names seem to change with the wind, at least the botanical ones do, and not all gardeners are plant savvy. But you don't need to be a botanist to grow plants for pollinators – all you need is a few pots and planters or a patch of garden.

For me the plants were my entry into the world of pollinators. It was the relationships that formed between plants and the insects that visited them that got me hooked. A simple way to see what plants are good for pollinators is to visit an open garden or watch which plants attract them in your neighbour's plot. Most people want to grow plants that are good for our butterflies and bees. You might want to grow herbs but

Planting for pollinators can take many forms. Generally the flowers are important, but many pollinators have offspring that need larval food plants. © Jean Vernon.

would rather choose those that will feed pollinators too. Or maybe you've got a small plot and want every plant to earn its place. You can also look at some of the images in this book and see the plants that the featured pollinators have been photographed on. You might start to notice a pattern of typical colours and of course flower shapes. Once you get the idea, your garden transformation is going to be much easier.

PICK OF THE PLANTS

I've picked great pollinator plants in different categories to get you started and help you choose what to grow. But it's not just about the flowers. Plants are the lowest layer of the food chain and many pollinators need particular plants to feed their caterpillar or larval stage too.

If you have a bigger area to plant then spend a bit of time visiting gardens near you at different times of the year and pay attention to those that are pollinator magnets (i.e. plants that attract lots of different insects). Use your ears as well as your eyes and home in on the buzz. I'm convinced the sound is healing; perhaps it resonates on a specific frequency but whatever it is I am truly hooked.

A POLLINATOR DAY OUT

Many gardens open to the public also sell plants, so look out for seasonal plants that the pollinators are visiting. The fact that the plants are thriving near to where you live usually indicates they should grow well in your garden too. That's important because some plants need particular conditions to grow well. Plants that are pollinator magnets really are providing good pollen and nectar for your local pollinator populations. Make a list of plants that are buzzing with insects, take photos and seek them out from a local nursery that can offer expert advice.

BE AWARE

It's not as simple as going to the garden centre to buy plants for pollinators. Unfortunately some plants available for sale may have been pre-treated with systemic chemicals (including the dreaded neonicotinoids) to keep them free from pests and diseases, and the really bad news is that the presence of these pesticides, even in very small doses can and does affect pollinator health. The best way to avoid this is to use an organic nursery that grows plants without the need for pesticides. It's easier to find organic edible plants that we might eat, e.g. fruit, herbs and vegetables, but the demand for organic ornamental plants is growing. There are some specialist organic plant nurseries out there, and even some that specifically sell plants for pollinators (Ref 85, 86, 87). Seek them out and support them, they are making a difference.

Grow from seed; this gives you a greater choice of plant varieties and more plants for your money, so it's ideal for sharing and increasing the bee friendly plants in and around your area. You can even share or give away excess seed to make the very most of every seed in every packet.

Take cuttings from pollinator plants and share them far and wide. If you've got a great plant that can be propagated, this is the ideal way to fill your garden with more pollinator plants and spread the love by giving them as gifts to fellow gardeners.

SPREAD THE WORD

Giving pollinator friendly plants as impromptu gifts is a great way to spread pollen and nectar rich plants. Even if the recipient isn't a pollinator fanatic, by planting your gift outside they are helping them. Encourage them to take cuttings or save seeds and give them away to their friends to keep the process going. Imagine it as a positive form of pyramid selling without the greed, without exchanging money and with the benefit and health of pollinators in mind. Make it into a fun project and see how far you can take it. Spreading the love of gardening, plants and nature benefits everyone. You can do it with seed too. Save seed from your favourite pollinator plants and pop them into thank you cards, birthday cards and any letters you might send. Keep a few for the Christmas crackers (and the Christmas card list) and take them to meetings to share with friends or anyone you think might grow them. If there's a seed swap near you, spread the pollinator love there and if you feel able and brave enough give a talk and share your passion.

Spread the message. Even people with little pollinator knowledge can help by planting the right plants if they have a garden, or even just a window box. Make it easy for them and share good pollinator plants.

EASY FROM SEED

Plants can seem expensive, especially if you have a garden to fill. But remember that each plant is an investment, choose wisely and plant well. But there is a way to cheat and fill your garden with colour and drama, and great pollinator plants very cost effectively. You can grow from seed. What's more you might be able to harvest self-sown seedlings or save seed from a friend's plot of great pollinator plants. Here are a few that are easy from seed and really good for your garden pollinators.

ATTRACTING GARDEN POLLINATORS

Viper's Bugloss (*Echium spp*)

There's one group of plants that are simply the very best for pollinators and especially bees and hoverflies. They can be grown from seed and they include a British native species that is really easy to grow. You might have seen the great spires of the giant viper's bugloss on your holidays in Cornwall or the Isle of Wight or in protected walled gardens around the UK. It's a fabulous plant with hundreds of nectar rich flowers in one place. It's not hardy in the UK, which is why you find it growing in more southern climes. Some sawfly larva will feed on these plants. Sawflies are also pollinators.

There is a winter hardy, UK native echium that grows wild in some places and is commonly called viper's bugloss. It is a biennial, which means that it doesn't flower until the second summer of its lifecycle, when it will flower, set seed and die. Usually these plants will self-seed all over the place each year, taking two years to reach maturity and flower. They will pop up in the gravel paths, between the paving and all over the place.

Great! Gently dig them up, pot them up and plant them all around the garden, making sure that you have plenty left to share with your garden buddies. Viper's bugloss flowers for months and is a magnet for all pollinators that collect the soft blue pollen and sugar rich nectar. You can grow it in pots where the shorter spires of rich blue flowers will fountain over the edges and look beautiful. If you only grow one plant for the pollinators this summer, make it an echium; you will be astounded by the different pollinators it attracts and will get flowers for weeks on end.

*The nectar rich flowers of viper's bugloss (*Echium vulgare*) feed a wide range of garden pollinators. © Jean Vernon.*

Borage (*Borago officinalis*)

Borage is an amazing pollinator plant. It's an annual herb worthy of any garden. The reason it's such a good pollinator plant and is so popular with insects is because its flowers replenish their nectaries regularly, every ten minutes or so (Ref 90), so it's an open all hours bar with generous supplies of the sugary nectar and making it a magnet for pollinators. It's also a food plant for Painted Lady caterpillars. Grow borage from seed, but once you've got it, it will self-seed around the garden. Look out for seed of white flowered borage, which is a pretty alternative.

Borage replenishes its nectaries regularly to entice pollinators like this leaf cutter bee, to its flowers. © Jean Vernon.

ATTRACTING GARDEN POLLINATORS

Cosmos (*Cosmos bipinnatus*)

If there's one summer flower that you can grow really easily from seed to attract garden pollinators that will also be a great cut flower and border stalwart, the cosmos has to be top of the list. It's the perfect flower for pollinators because it has flat, open, dinner plate kind of daisy-like flowers, with pollen and nectar rich centres and plenty of room for several insects at a time.

These are great garden plants with masses of flowers from June to October. You can buy garden ready plants after the last frost in mid to late spring, or buy a packet or two of seeds. Choose the easy to grow *Cosmos bipinnatus* in a mix of single open flowers and sow the seeds in mid April onwards into pots of good quality seed compost, sprinkle the seed thinly over the surface and cover with a thin layer of compost. Germinate in a frost-free place and plant out after the last frost has passed.

Cosmos flowers last into later summer and are beautiful garden plants. © *Jean Vernon*

Sunflowers (*Helianthus spp*)

Every garden should have a few sunflowers, if only for the fact that they make fabulous food plants for pollinators and wildlife. But who can resist their sunny, smiley faces?

These easy to grow plants can be grown from seed and used to encourage the kids into giant sunflower competitions and more. Some moths and beetles lay their eggs around the roots of sunflower plants and caterpillars of the Painted Lady butterfly and the Garden Tiger moth may feed on sunflower leaves.

Not all sunflowers are tall with giant flowers; some are compact with many heads and ideal for growing in containers, while others have orange, red or even white flowers. But it is the yellow ones that are thought to be more attractive to the many pollinating insects. Sunflowers are grown *en masse* for their oil and their seeds,  both for birdseed and sunflower oil production. But in the garden it is the pollen rich flowers that attract many pollinators. The centre of the flower is made up of hundreds of tiny tubular flowers, ideal for a feast on what is in effect the perfect landing pad. An insect can zoom in and then spend the day supping nectar from each individual tube, or collecting the rich yellow pollen. Without pollinators there would be no sunflower seeds and no sunflower oil. And yet sunflowers were one of the agricultural crops where the seed was treated with systemic insecticides (neonicotinoids) before planting. When they have finished flowering the seed heads will feed the birds and the hollow stems can be cut, dried and used in homemade insect houses or left *in situ* for the pollinators.

Sunflowers are easy to grow and a great choice to grow for wildlife. © Jean Vernon.

ATTRACTING GARDEN POLLINATORS

Nasturtium (*Tropaeolum spp*)

If you want a plant that's really easy to grow and is edible and a great pollinator plant too, nasturtiums are a really good choice. They are incredibly easy to grow from seed and once you've established them on your plot they will usually self-seed. Sow the large seeds in pots of seed compost anytime from mid spring and about five weeks before the last spring frost. Keep the pots in a light frost-free place. A windowsill or greenhouse is ideal and when they germinate keep turning the pots twice a day to prevent the seedlings getting too leggy. If you are wary of sowing seeds, don't be, nasturtiums are a great plant to start with and you'll get dozens of plants for the price of one packet of seed. You may find pots of germinated seedlings at the garden centre. Either way your young plants can be planted into pots and containers outdoors after the last frost. You can also sow seeds direct into the garden soil from May onwards. Most of the nasturtium varieties that we grow in the UK are annuals, which means you sow and grow them over the course of one long season and they flower and set seed the same year. Plants will be killed off by the first hard frost of autumn, but each one will flower for weeks on end. Nasturtiums are also larval plants for the cabbage white butterflies and can be grown as a decoy to protect your brassicas.

One of the great things about nasturtiums is that the leaves, flowers and seeds are edible. You can add the leaves to salads, especially useful in spring when your homegrown salad supplies may be low.

When the plants are growing strongly you can make a tasty peppery hot pesto from the leaves and you can even add the flowers to stir-fries, or to salads too for extra colour and drama to your menus. Do leave as many as you can for the pollinators though. There's nothing nicer than watching our giant bumblebees literally climb inside these flowers in search of nectar. The bright coloured flowers are like flags to pollinators, advertising their rich, sugary nectar source to entice them in to the deep flowers.

The long tongued Garden bumblebee can climb inside nasturtiums to feed. © Martin Mulchinock.

HERBS FOR POLLINATORS

If you are new to gardening a good place to start is by growing herbs. Many herbs are perennial and some are shrubs, so once you've got them growing they will get bigger and better year on year. But the great thing about herbs is that you get fresh flavour for your summer menus; some make fabulous herb tea and your pollinators get plenty of nectar too. Many herbs are also important butterfly and moth caterpillar plants.

Marjoram 'Origanum vulgare'

If there's one herb you really should grow for pollinators it is marjoram. It is so easy to grow, it's a great ingredient for summer menus and it has very nectar rich flowers that attract many garden pollinators. It's a perennial with pretty pale pink or white flowers. In summer the flower heads attract hoverflies, bees, flies and wasps as well as butterflies and moths. It is also a larval food plant for mint moth caterpillars.

One of the best herbs to grow for pollinators is the wild marjoram. It self seeds and flowers profusely. © Jean Vernon.

Rosemary (*Salvia rosmarinus*)

This is one of my favourite herbs. First of all it is evergreen, keeping its richly fragrant leaves through the depths of winter. This means there are always rosemary leaves to add to your winter menus, make herbal tea and lift your spirits on the darkest days with its wonderful uplifting fragrance. Rosemary is a really good pollinator plant.

The nectar rich flowers are a magnet for spring pollinators, searching for sustenance. In a sheltered spot rosemary plants can flower through late winter and into early spring, provide vital forage for pollinators out of season.

It loves a hot dry spot with well-drained soil and once established it will flower and produce its fabulous aromatic leaves.

Rosemary often flowers in late winter and into spring. Its nectar rich flowers are vital for pollinators on the wing.
© Jean Vernon.

Thyme (*Thymus spp*)

Thyme flowers are a great source of nectar for our garden pollinators and it is also a very useful culinary plant; its leaves are tasty and strong in flavor and used in a variety of savoury dishes. But thyme is also hailed as an extremely powerful medicinal plant. Renowned for its antimicrobial, antifungal and anti parasitic properties thyme has a unique history as a heal-all plant.

Bees have been shown to seek out plants like thyme for their medicinal properties to self medicate and heal themselves by feeding on the nectar enriched with medicinal properties (Ref 91). The Large Blue butterfly lays its eggs on wild thyme.

Mint (*Mentha spp*)

One of the easiest plants to grow in a pot for pollinators is garden mint. It is well suited to container growing because mint plants spread by making rhizomes that grow sideways from the plants, creating the spreading pattern that it is so well known for. Some gardeners regard mint as a bit of a thug if planted into a border. You could look at it like that, but I prefer to think of it as a very prolific and successful filler in the border, that will not only generate masses and masses of herb tea material (and believe me there is nothing nicer than freshly made mint herb tea from the garden) but will also produce spires of soft pink and mauve flowers that are rich in nectar for our garden pollinators.

Mint is a great plant for beginners because it's easy to grow and you can take cuttings from it with little effort and give them to new homeowners, youngsters and hipsters to get them growing. It's the first step on the road not just to gardening but to supporting pollinators too. The mint moth needs members of the mint family to feed its caterpillars.

There are dozens of mints you could choose to grow, but if a good mint herbal tea is your quest you can't go wrong with Moroccan or Spanish mint; seek them out, or find a mint that you like the smell and taste of and start a collection.

Sage (*Salvia officinalis*)

You might be surprised that the herbal sage plants also flower. Many growers will pinch out the flower spikes to generate more of the delicious leaves, but I like to let my sage plants bloom. The blossoms are the softest mauve and rich in nectar. They are pollinator magnets and will attract a variety of long-tongued bees, butterflies, moths and flies, but they are also of the victim of nectar robbers that will nibble a hole close to the nectar source and drink the nectar through the hole, and secondary nectar robbers that take advantage of the easy access to the nectar.

The mauve flowers of sage are popular with pollinators. Bombus lapidarius supping nectar. © Jean Vernon.

Sage is a woody shrub and can become a leggy, sprawling bush but it's a fantastic culinary herb with fragrant leaves and of course has many close relatives that are wonderful ornamental plants (the salvias). Let the stems flower for pollinator food and then cut off the spent flower heads to tidy the plant and encourage new shoots and leaves. Take cuttings in summer when the plant is strong and healthy, root them in a gritty compost and overwinter in a cold greenhouse or coldframe. Choose the standard herb sage, or some of its cultivars for the best flowers; the plants tend to be stronger growing and flower more readily than the variegated, purple or tricolor sage. And don't forget the many ornamental types of salvia that are rich in nectar and are great forage plants for the long-tongued pollinators.

Chives (*Allium schoenoprasum*)

If you've just got a small pot to plant up, choose to grow garden chives. They are easy to grow, come back year after year and flower with attractive mauve clusters of flowers in early summer, which provide nectar for wasps, bees, hoverflies, butterflies and moths. And of course you can snip the leaves to add some flavour and colour to your sandwiches and salads. They are great for growing in a pot and a good way to start growing a few ingredients for your menus.

VEGETABLE PLANTS FOR POLLINATORS

Without pollinators we would not have many of our favourite vegetables. Around one third of the food that we eat depends on pollination, and that includes food plants grown for livestock, as well as the flowering and fruiting plants we grow in our gardens and on our allotments. Many of our vegetable plants provide pollen and nectar for pollinators and then go on to produce a harvest of something fresh and delicious for our menus. But even the plants that we don't normally allow to flower can offer forage for our buzzy friends. Carrots and parsnips left in the ground will flower in their second year, creating essential, nectar rich flowers for the hoverflies, flies and bees of all sorts. Lettuce, chicory and coriander that run to seed can be allowed to flower for the pollinators. Even the broccoli that has gone past the point of harvest will flower and offer its bright yellow flowers to the insects. As will leeks, onions and even garlic, pushing up attractive flower heads rich in nectar for pollinators. So leave a few vegetable plants to flower and provide nectar and pollen for pollinators. You might also be able to save the seed and sow it next year.

Runner Beans (*Phaseolus coccineus*)

Some of my favourite home grown veg are runner beans. They are really easy to grow from seed. You can train them up wigwams of sticks and canes so they don't need a massive amount of space, and these climbing, twining plants then flower. The flowers are a magnet for pollinators and especially some of the larger bumblebees that climb inside the flowers in search of nectar, pollinating the flowers as they go. Without these pollinators you would not get your crop of tender runner beans. There are dozens of great varieties, some with white flowers, but most with red. Sow a few extra seeds in June for a late crop of tender pods. Delicious.

If you only grow one vegetable this year grow a wigwam of runner beans. They look great, produce lots of tasty pods and are essential food for bumblebees. © Martin Mulchinock.

Courgette (*Cucurbita pepo*)

You don't need many courgette plants to provide for a family of four all summer. In fact, just two or three plants will keep you in courgettes for weeks on end. They are a hugely versatile crop that can be baked, stir fried or even spiralised as low calorie noodles.

The large yellow flowers attract pollinators into their depths, seeking out the bright yellow pollen. In the US they have a squash bee that pretty much only feeds on the pollen of these plants, but in the UK they are visited by many types of pollinators, small and large.

Courgette flowers are male or female and open in sequence. Large pollinators can move pollen between flowers of different plants. © Martin Mulchinock.

Leek (*Allium porrum*)

Most people don't think of leeks as flowering plants, but if you leave a handful in the ground over winter and allow them to grow well into the next growing year you will be surprised by the tall flower spike full of pinky mauve and white flowers that forms. Leeks belong to the allium family and are related to those ornamental purple balls that gardeners grow for late spring interest.

With lots of nectar rich flowers in close proximity the flower head of leeks can become vital forage and are popular with some solitary bees, flies and other pollinators.

Pea (*Pisum sativum*)

Another easy to grow vegetable that flowers early and then forms pods in early summer are the peas. Most of the pea family, including clover, sweet peas and vetches are popular with the long tongued pollinators. This includes the humble pea, or if you prefer, the

Alliums of all sorts are rich in nectar and important pollinator plants. © Jean Vernon.

very closely related mange tout. When it comes to the edible pea types the flowers provide vital food for our pollinating friends and we get the sweet, yummy peas and pea shoots to eat. Please note the ornamental peas are not edible in any form!

Broad Bean (*Vicia faba*)

If you've only ever eaten woolly broad beans it's time to start again. Grow your own, let them flower for the pollinators and pick the pods young when the beans inside are fresh and tender. Stir fry them or cook with cream cheese and serve with pasta. Delicious. And the pollinators will love the extra source of nectar in spring. Easy to grow, sow them in the autumn for an earlier crop or sow in spring. You can even eat the leaves in salads.

CLIMBERS FOR POLLINATORS

Make the most of the vertical surfaces in your garden as they offer an extra area to grow more plants for pollinators. Walls and fences can be fitted with cross wires or a trellis to support a range of flowering plants that clamber and climb. Here are five good ones.

Red Jasmine (*Jasminum beesianum*)

Just like the scientific name suggests this is a really good bee plant. But it's also good for other pollinators too. It flowers in late May and June and is a mass of dusky pink/red flowers that are simply a magnet for nectaring insects. It's a rampant climber and will quickly cover a trellis or arch with masses of tiny green leaves on twining leafy stems that grasp and grip any support. Really easy to grow, perfect for covering up a corner or an eyesore if you give it something to clamber through, though it can get top heavy and does tend to become bare towards the bottom after a few years.

Ivy (*Hedera helix*)

You might be surprised to find wild ivy on the list of choice pollinator plants but it is an excellent autumn source of food and attractive to a wide range of wild pollinators and of course especially important for the Ivy bee. Stake out the flowers and see what feeds there and you will find all sorts of flies, wasps, hornets, hoverflies and even butterflies

ATTRACTING GARDEN POLLINATORS

and bees feeding on the flowers. Ivy is ideal for covering over an old shed or wall at the bottom of the garden where it can be allowed to flower. Keep it under control and don't let it take over. It's a larval food plant for the Holly Blue butterfly and the black berries that form are good for the birds too.

Honeysuckle (*Lonicera periclymenum*)

Native plants are often hailed as being better for pollinators, though they don't seem to mind just as long as they can get to the nectar and pollen. Honeysuckle in its purest form is a native wildflower of the hedgerows and a good plant for pollinators, but there are some lovely garden cultivars which are also very good, such as the Tellman's honeysuckle with its vibrant orange flowers.

Honeysuckles have long tubular flowers that are mostly better for the long tongued pollinators such as the Garden bumblebee, moths, butterflies and also the Carder bees. When the nectar is plentiful shorter tongued pollinators can access it, often after a rain shower when the plants have replenished the nectaries. It's also a food plant for the White Admiral caterpillars. And don't forget the winter honeysuckle it's not a climber but it's an essential winter pollinator plant.

Clothe a wall with a flowering honeysuckle. This golden orange species is Lonicera tellmanniana. © Jean Vernon.

Alpine Clematis (*Clematis alpina*)

Some of the garden clematis are especially attractive to our pollinators. In spring when the *Clematis alpina* flowers hang like dancing fairies in blousy purple skirts they are often buzzing with the bumblebee queens searching for food. An established plant with many flowers is a great source of forage for garden pollinators, especially if they have nested nearby and don't need to fly far to reach your plants. There are a few forms of *Clematis alpina* to transform your trellis and archways in a range of beautiful shades of pink, purple and white. Choose one or two and marry with a later flowering *Clematis macropetala* to extend the flowering season and food supply for pollinators. Some clematis are food plants for the Angle Shade moth caterpillars.

Perennial Sweet Pea (*Lathyrus latifolius*)

Many of the pea family are great pollinators' plants and that includes the runner beans and the sweet peas, but this plant, the perennial sweet pea is a really good choice for lots of reasons. First it's hardy, easy to grow and a prolific flowerer. It's a caterpillar plant for the exotic Long-Tailed Blue butterfly. In my garden it's a favourite forage plant for the leaf-cutter bees and the Common Carder bee, which busily force themselves

inside the flowers in search of pollen and nectar. To keep it flowering it is essential to remove the spent blooms and any forming seed pods, which incidentally are NOT edible and should not be eaten. There are several colour forms of this plant: a white and soft pink and also a vibrant fuchsia pink form. Well worth growing and a really tough, good climber for bees and other pollinators.

For some Leaf-cutter action plant the perennial sweet pea. This little bee has pollen packed on her scopa.
© Jean Vernon.

POLLINATOR PLANTS FOR POTS
AND HANGING BASKETS

If you've only got a balcony or window box, you need to choose plants that will thrive and work hard in this restricted space. Several pots and planters grouped together can be planted with all sorts of flowering plants that will offer you a pretty focal point and the pollinators a source of food. Keep your pots and baskets well-fed during the growing season, and choose an organic feed for flowering plants to keep them blooming for longer. Remember that to make plenty of nectar your plants need water, so keep your pots and containers well-watered.

There are dozens of great plants for pollinators that you can grow in pots and containers, including some of the perennials, shrubs and annuals mentioned before. So if the plants you like aren't on my list that doesn't mean they are not a good choice.

Lavender (*Lavandula angustifolia*)

Every garden should have lavender. Whether it's just a pot with a compact variety, or a dividing hedge, this plant comes in a wide range of shapes and forms and is fantastic for us and for our pollinators. Generally attractive to the longer-tongued pollinators including many bumblebees, butterflies and moths.

Perennial Wall Flowers (*Erysimum ssp*)

This is a great plant for summer pots and containers because it flowers for weeks and weeks and weeks and because it is a magnet for our pollinator friends. My favourite is 'Bowles Mauve' which as the name suggests has rich purple flowers. It can get a bit straggly, so prune gently to keep in check and take cuttings from the pieces you cut off.

Perennial wallflowers (Erysimum spp) *are great plants for pollinators, like this Hairy-footed Flower bee. © Liam Olds.*

Bidens (*Bidens spp*)

Bidens are a lovely basket and container plant. There are several types with names like 'Bees Dance' and 'Bees Alive' which are not just beautiful but the flowers smell of honey and attract the bees. If you've got more room then consider a perennial type like the beautiful cream flowered *Bidens aurea*, perfect for the middle or the back of the border and a favourite of hoverflies.

The perennial bidens aurea is a beautiful perennial plant and good for hoverflies like this Eristalis spp. © *Jean Vernon.*

ATTRACTING GARDEN POLLINATORS

Fuchsia (*Fuchsia magellanica*)

There are many great reasons to grow fuchsias. The dangling fairyesque flowers are spectacular. There are hardy varieties that you can keep from year to year (and grow in the flower border). You can take cuttings very easily of these plants to share with friends and they are very, very rich in nectar. It does take a long tongued pollinator to get to the nectaries, but these flowers are also robbed by short-tongued bees chewing holes above the nectary. Fuchsias are a food plant for the spectacular Elephant Hawk moth caterpillar.

Fuchsia flowers are rich in nectar. This buff-tailed bumblebee is nectar robbing. © Jean Vernon.

Bird's Foot Trefoil (*Lotus corniculatus*)

This is an incredible plant for all sorts of pollinators and it's very pretty too. It's one of the pea family and has bright yellow slipper-shaped flowers, which are sometimes tinged with red. It's a native wildflower and often found growing in wild grassland. You might have it in your lawn. It's a caterpillar plant for several moth species. Its flowers are very rich in nectar. It's also a perennial. You can buy seed and plug plants online and they would work really well in a hanging basket.

Ring the changes and plant wildflowers in pots and containers. Bird's foot trefoil works well in a planter. © Jean Vernon.

Spring Flowering Bulbs

Mark the start of spring with a pot of crocus bulbs, grape hyacinths, dwarf tulips or snowdrops. Either buy them in flower from an organic plant nursery or buy organic bulbs mail order in early autumn and plant them immediately, leaving the pots outside for the winter. The bulbs will start to sprout in winter and then flower, providing pollen and nectar for early emerging pollinators. They could also be grown in hanging baskets. After flowering, remove the dead flowers; the leaves will die back to the level of the compost and the bulbs will regrow to flower again next spring.

A small pot of spring flowering crocus will help feed queen bumblebees. © Jean Vernon.

ATTRACTING GARDEN POLLINATORS

EARLY SPRING PERENNIALS FOR POLLINATORS

Late winter and early spring are the most critical times for pollinators, whether it's the overwintering honeybees first venturing out on a sunny day or the emerging queens and solitary bees, butterflies and hoverflies. Once the weather starts to warm the garden comes alive with pollinators searching for food. The trouble is that the weather can be very unpredictable and a warm spell that lures our insect friends from their torpor can just as quickly turn to cold. Unless there are sufficient nectar and pollen rich flowers for these early risers to forage on they are in deep trouble. Even plants that are naturally up and flowering in winter can stop providing nectar and pollen in a cold snap, especially when covered in snow or hard frost. Establish a handful of great garden perennials that are also good pollinator plants to sustain your winter active insects. Once your clumps are mature you can experiment by forcing part of a plant with cloches for earlier flowers, leaving the rest to their natural flowering time, or pot up cuttings and bring them on in the greenhouse so that when they flower you can place them outside for the emerging pollinators. These five perennials will bridge the gap from winter into spring and provide for garden pollinators for several weeks or months until spring starts in earnest.

Hellebores (*Helleborus spp*)

Hellebores are almost designed for pollinators with their nodding flowers and virtually bottomless nectaries to attract our insect friends. Research from the University of Bristol (Ref 92) measured the nectar in spring flowers and discovered that one hellebore flower provided the same amount of nectar as 157 snowdrop flowers! The large bell shaped hellebore flowers create living umbrella-like shelters for the feeding insects in poor weather and there's a wide range of species that flower from Christmas right into spring, offering your wild pollinators a generous menu of energy rich nectar to get them going. These elegant flowers are a vital resource and each one keeps its nectaries provisioned for up to three weeks, making these plants excellent for emerging pollinators including the queen bumblebees, queen wasps, hoverflies and other wild bees as well as the honeybees. What's more the flowers contain plenty of protein rich pollen, essential for feeding the developing brood of wild bees and honeybees early in the season.

Hellebores have become an on-trend plant for many plant enthusiasts and some varieties and strains change hands for a lot of money, but pollinators aren't bothered how much your plants cost, so if your main reason for planting hellebores is to sustain garden pollinators you can buy cheaper, unnamed seedlings from plant sales and allow them to self-seed. Share them and give them as gifts; the little seedlings will take

In spring, hellebores are an abundant source of nectar. © Martin Mulchinock.

two to three years to flower, and who knows, you might have bred your own beautiful strain, but as long as your plants flower and provide copious pollen and nectar for pollinators that's what really matters.

Lungwort (*Pulmonaria spp*)

Lungwort is a great late winter, early spring plant for pollinators. It's low growing and available in different forms; the most common is often called lords and ladies due to its pink and blue flowers. The leaves are often spotted and slightly hairy but it's the early spring nectar rich flowers appearing in February and March that attract early emerging pollinators.

Pulmonaria is a slow spreader forming cushions of leaves and flowers in low growing clumps. Let it grow and spread and if you are lucky you will attract one of the prettiest solitary bees that seems to have a preference for its flowers. The Hairy-footed Flower bees simply love lungwort; in fact it's a good way to spot them as they hover around pulmonarias in flower, darting about like hummingbirds and barely stopping long enough to feed. It's a woodland plant so it tolerates some shade.

For a pretty plant that supports early emerging pollinators, grow lungwort. © Jean Vernon.

It's also a favourite of bee flies, some moths and the queen bumbles that emerge in spring and start to provision their nests.

Perennial Borage (*Trachystemon orientalis*)

Don't be put off by the botanical name of this plant. It is also known as perennial or oriental borage and that's a very fair description. It's closely related to borage and it's a fantastic winter flowering source of nectar for early pollinators. To be honest it rarely features on pollinator plant lists and that's a real puzzle. I first came across it growing with snowdrops at a open garden day. It was flowering on a bank and took my attention as it was buzzing with bees (as were the snowdrops) but I had no idea what it was. Some years later I found it at a nursery in spring, recognised it and bought a pot. The rest, as they say is history, but it's a must-have pollinator plant and a good garden doer but only if you have the space. Plus it's perennial so once you've planted it; it will come up year after year.

The only downside is that it does spread. It's not uncontrollable and quite honestly it's such a great plant I wouldn't let that put you off. You can keep it under control by dividing it regularly even if you grow it in a large planter and then give away the divisions, which would be a fantastic gift for any pollinator friendly gardener.

It flowers when there is so little else in flower in the garden. Depending on the weather it can start to flower anytime from December through to March. It likes a shady or semi shady spot (but tolerates sun too) and it has clusters of soft mauve and white flowers that look very much like borage flowers with the petals turned back.

Beg a rhizome/root of this pollinator magnet. It's a bit of a tongue twister, but commonly known as perennial or oriental borage. © Martin Mulchinock.

Comfrey (*Symphytum spp*)

This is another great perennial pollinator plant better suited to larger gardens and allotments because it spreads. But it flowers quite early in the season, sometimes flowering as early as January. It's perfect for long-tongued bumblebees as they build their colonies and if the naughty short-tongued bumbles have chewed into the back of the flower then shorter tongued insects can feed on it too. It's really worth their while as comfrey is another plant that keeps its nectaries fully loaded with nectar. It replenishes them every 40 minutes so it's a reliable nectar bar. Comfrey keeps on flowering and if you cut it back it will grow back and flower some more. It's a larval food plant for the Garden Tiger moth caterpillar. What's more it's easy to split and share with your gardening buddies and it's a really valuable plant for other reasons too. Traditional gardeners use comfrey leaves to make an all-natural plant food for their plants. They fill large watertight containers with the leaves and then add rainwater, allowing the leaves to steep and rot down into a pungent, but nitrogen-rich plant food that some refer to as compost tea. You can also compost the leaves within a compost bin to add vital nutrients to the resulting soil conditioner, which once added to your garden soil will improve the soil health and increase the beneficial microbe count.

Add comfrey leaves to your compost heap but let it flower for the bees. © Jean Vernon.

Some comfrey grows tall with racemes of flowers, while others are more ground cover plants. There are lots of forms and plenty of hybrids and it's very easy to grow. Comfrey plants can be contained in a large planter, but they can be a bit of a thug, so be warned. You can divide the plants and share them, and of course harvest the leaves for fertiliser, but this is a true survivor and once you've got it in the garden it's there to stay. There are several different types with a range of flower colours. I love the stunning cobalt blue flowers of *Symphytum* 'Hidcote Blue'. Find a friend who has some and beg a piece to grow in your garden, but make sure that you like the one that they have and that you plant it somewhere where it will get some sunshine and can run (spread) a little.

Mountain Cornflower (*Centaurea montana*)

This is a reliable spring flowerer in my garden and a magnet for all early active pollinators, bumblebees, wasps and especially carder bees. It's really easy to grow and also spreads itself around, gently producing stems topped with the most beautiful rich deep blue cornflowers. It's so pretty you could cut it for the house, but then you deprive your pollinators of its pollen and nectar. In a warm spring it can flower in April and then if you dead head and cut it back hard (once it's established of course) it will grow back and flower again giving a second crop of its fabulous flowers.

GREAT SUMMER PERENNIALS FOR POLLINATORS

The best thing about garden perennials is that they come back year after year and get bigger and better each season. You can plant three or five of one type together and they will grow into a healthy swath of plants that will provide efficient forage for your wild pollinators. When choosing good plants for pollinators be aware of the June gap when there is a big dip in the flowers available for our insect friends.

Lamb's Ears (*Stachys byzantina*)

There are so many reasons to grow this plant. First it's really great for children, because it has beautiful, silvery grey, soft furry leaves. In fact it is probably the very first plant that I fell in love with as a child. It's easy to grow and is a good ground cover plant. But when it flowers it sends up tremendous soft silver grey flower turrets that are softly seasoned with pale pink flowers in whorls. It's a good plant for many pollinators as the flowers are accessible, but it is known for attracting the fascinating Wool carder bee,

ATTRACTING GARDEN POLLINATORS

which uses the fluff from the leaves to line its nest. Here the males hang out waiting for their queen and they will chase off anything else that dares to cross the border into their territory. It's fun to watch and a great way to learn about this species of bee.

It's in the mint family and a favourite plant for the Forked-tailed Flower bee that feeds on the nectar rich flowers, as do butterflies and moths.

If I had a top five bee plants list, this would be in there: lamb's ears (Stachys byzantina). © Jean Vernon.

Catmint (*Nepeta spp*)

Catmint is a not just a lure for the feline species, it's also a crowd puller when it comes to pollinators. It's a perennial that dies back in winter to ground level, to spring up again as the lighter evenings arrive around the spring equinox. There are dozens of varieties, but Nepeta 'Six Hills Giant' is a popular choice, with long racemes of

purple flowers. It's a great plant for pollinators and a beautiful garden plant in its own right. It's another member of the mint family and a caterpillar plant for the pretty Mint moth. If you have local cats, protect the emerging spring shoots from their attention. My lovely old ginger tom George used to sit on it in spring and roll around in the tender shoots, which didn't grow too well after that. An upturned empty hanging basket is good protection until the shoots are long enough and prolific enough to resist feline attention. If you remove the flowers as they finish, many plants will produce a second crop that will provide late summer forage for pollinators. If you have a large clump then snip the tops out of some of the stems at the front and they will flower a bit later than the first flush of flowers extending the flowering season. You can dry the leaves to make little catnip toys for cat lovers and their cats.

There are so many great pollinator plants in the mint family. Cat mint (Nepeta spp) is a really good one. © Jean Vernon.

Bugle (*Ajuga spp*)

This is a great ground cover perennial plant and another member of the mint family. There are many good garden worthy varieties. One of my favourites is the larger leaved 'Catlin's Giant'. It has fabulous purple black glossy leaves and produces beautiful spires of purple blue flowers in late spring that attract and feed garden pollinators. It can grow around and under garden shrubs, flowering before they fill out and block the daylight. Once you've got it, it is very easy to take cuttings from its runners and share with gardening friends.

Dead Nettles (*Lamium spp*)

There are lots of great varieties of this woodland plant, which is in the mint family and has leaves that look like nettles but without the fiery sting. The hooded orchid like flowers form in a circle around the stem at leaf nodes and can be bright yellow, creamy white, pink, purple or bronze depending on the species you choose to grow. Some make good ground cover and will spread or form clumps. The nectar rich flowers are important for pollinators. One of my favourites is the bronze flowered *Lamium orvala* that has rich green leaves. But there are several forms with very attractive silver splashed foliage like *Lamium maculatum*.

Another member of the mint family, dead nettles have nectar rich flowers and are great ground cover. © Jean Vernon.

Geranium 'Rozanne'

This is a hardy geranium, more commonly known as a cranesbill. Unlike many of these plants, this one is sterile, it doesn't set seed, but it does make copious amounts of nectar and it has lots of flowers, which makes it a great pollinator plant. Good for containers, or let it scramble through the flowerbed.

Giant Hyssop (*Agastache spp*)

Giant hyssop is not the same as the herb hyssop; its proper name is agastache (it's in the mint family) and it's a real winner with pollinators. Look out for plants at the garden centre or grow it from seed if you are seed sower. 'Black Adder' is the one I grow and it is commonly available. It's also a perennial, so once planted and established

it's there pretty much for good (and if you are lucky it will self-seed too). It's a great garden plant with spikes of smoky purple flowers all summer and it's even got slightly aromatic foliage too that you can use to make tea, though I must confess I haven't tried it. There's a liquorice-scented variety called the Anise agastache for tea if you like that flavour; I don't. But best of all, agastache are pretty resistant to garden pests and a powerful magnet for longer-tongued pollinators like butterflies and especially carder bees.

There are plenty of other great forms of this plant with pink, white, rich mauve and

Look out for fresh newly emerged virgin queen bumblebees feeding on agastache in late summer. © Jean Vernon.

softer blue flower spikes and it's really easy to grow. It likes a sunny spot in the garden and will attract butterflies and other pollinators too. Grow it in a sunny border or in mixed perennial planter display for nectar rich flowers from mid-summer right through to autumn.

Sea Holly (*Eryngium planum*)

This is a great garden plant and an ideal pollinator plant with dozens of tiny flowers all clustered together in the central flower boss (the middle of the flower). Surprisingly this is in the carrot family (Apiaceae)! The flowers have attractive bracts and are good landing pads for pollinators especially the shorter-tongued hoverflies, flies, wasps and solitary bees. It's easy to grow and also good for cut flowers. It grows well in hot weather and well-drained sunny places. There are several forms of this plant that are all great pollinator plants. Plant them in clumps for the best effect. Once the plants establish they may self-seed and the clumps will mature into strong healthy plants.

Veronica spicata

The veronica genus offers a few forms but it is the upright, clump forming types that are actually the most fantastic pollinator plants. *Veronica spicata*, like the name suggests, has upright spikes of many flowers in dusky pinks, rich mauves and purple and soft whites. I'll leave it to you to choose which one is best for your garden; just know that they are all great for pollinators. It's sometimes called royal candles, you can see why, as the regal flower spikes, especially when purple, do look a bit like rich, verdant tapering candles of high quality that might adorn a royal feast. Fortunately these royal candles are available to buy to adorn your flowerbeds and feed garden pollinators. There is also a closely related plant called veronicastrum that is also great for pollinators, it grows a bit taller but is a very good nectar plant.

LATER SUMMER POLLINATOR PLANTS

You might think that summer was a time of plenty for pollinator plants, but actually it can be a blip in the calendar. There is a known 'June gap' where the availability of pollen and nectar rich plants dips. The Chelsea Chop can keep plants flowering longer spreading out the opening hours of essential pollinator diners. But there are several great stalwart plants that will help keep your pollinators perky. Look out for the daisy family, which include knapweeds, heleniums, rudbeckia, asters and echinacea.

Purple coneflower (*Echinacea spp*)

You may have encountered this plant in your quest to keep your immune system healthy. It's a common herbal supplement to protect against cold and flu. But its also a beautiful and perennial garden plant and available in several different forms. I love the fairyesque *Echinacea pallida* flowers, but there are also some very beautiful white forms. The important bit is the honey scented central boss that offers dozens of tiny flowers and a safe landing pad for your pollinator pals. Favoured by butterflies, bees and hoverflies, each flower lasts for weeks and is supported on strong stems. They belong to the daisy family, which are generally great pollinator plants; they are hardy and love a sunny spot in your garden.

Keep the borders flowering into autumn with a few late flowering perennials like echinacea. © Jean Vernon.

Black-eyed Susan (*Rudbeckia spp*)

Closely related to echinacea the rudbeckias are a fabulous, bright addition to the pollinator garden. Gorgeous yellow and orange petals surround the velvet brown centres. The petals are almost luminous in their vibrancy and a bright lure to direct insects to the nectar and pollen rich centres. There are lots of perennial and annual forms that will add important forage to your borders.

Michaelmas Daisies (*Aster amellus*)

Asters are fabulous late summer flowering plants. They love a sunny spot and are really tough and easy to grow. There's a lovely range of colours including purples and mauves, which seem particularly attractive to butterflies. Asters are in the daisy family and flower right into autumn providing vital late forage for garden pollinators before they start to overwinter.

ATTRACTING GARDEN POLLINATORS

Fill gaps in the late summer border with pollen and nectar rich asters. © Jean Vernon.

Purple top (*Verbena bonariensis*)

Verbena bonariensis is a great choice for gardens and for pollinators. It has airy see-through stems with purple flowers that mingle perfectly with other border perennials. A good strong clump of verbena will bear rafts of tiny flowers all clustered together in an easily accessible mass, creating a landing pad atop the tall wiry stems.

It's a great pollinator plant for long-tongued insects. It is also a butterfly magnet and will attract a wide variety of these beautiful ethereal creatures.

Leave the seed heads on the plant at the end of the summer, for this plant is yet another of the great self-seeders, spreading itself widely into gravel paths and nooks and crannies and of course into the garden soil. Buy one plant and get it established

The tall airy stems of Verbena bonariensis *are a landing pad for pollinators such as this hoverfly* (Eristalis arbustorum). © *Jean Vernon.*

so that it self-seeds. But for the very best value for money these plants are really easy to grow from seed for lots and lots of plants, which you can divide up and plant *en masse* in your garden and share with friends.

Ice Plant (*Sedum spp*)

The pollinator friendly ice plant (*Sedum spectabile,* now called *Hylotelephium spectabile*) is a real autumn stalwart, flowering right into the cooler months of the year. It has flat heads of flowers that are particularly attractive to butterflies, hoverflies and bees and become a vital source of nectar into autumn.

The common pink ice plant, as it is known, is a good garden plant, but for something a little more dramatic choose the rich purple red 'Purple Emperor' or 'Matrona' with softer purple succulent leaves. As winter approaches the drying flower heads look amazing crusted with frost and linger into the winter, creating interest in the border and helping to protect the emerging shoots in spring. The plants have succulent leaves and like a hot sunny spot in the garden.

Dahlia (*Dahlia spp*)

For lots of summer colour plant dahlia corms into pots and containers in spring. Choose the single, or open flowered varieties where the pollen and nectar is accessible to the pollinators. They need to be kept well fed and watered for the best display and when the plants have died back for the winter they need to be stored in a frost-free place for the winter and then potted up and protected until the last frost of spring has passed.

For cut flowers for the house and food plates for pollinators, Dahlias are a great choice. Seen her with Marmalade hoverflies. © Jean Vernon.

FRUIT FOR POLLINATORS

Let's be honest, most of us want or need a few edible plants in our gardens. But what if it were possible to have a sumptuous harvest of delicious fruit and provide a generous source of food for pollinators too? Well it is. You can have your fruit and eat it with these easy to grow types of fruit in your garden.

Raspberries (*Rubus spp*)

Raspberries are fantastic plants for pollinators. And they are extremely easy to grow and very productive plants for producing lots of fruit.

Raspberries are not just the most sumptuous and easy to grow garden fruit that there is, they feed the pollinators too. A bowl of sun-warmed, freshly picked raspberries with vanilla infused cream or ice cream is enough to make me pack up work for the day. Divine.

The bees think so too, but that's because the flowers are heavy with nectar and the canes are heavy with flowers. My raspberry patch buzzes with life in late May and June, with the sound of contented insects harvesting raspberry nectar for their stores.

If you are tight on space you can grow raspberries in a large container, or in a clump tied in to a central support. Just grow them. You won't be disappointed. And if you've got plenty of room let the raspberries grow rampant; they will run and spread around, but you'll be rewarded with fabulous fruit for pies and puddings, jams and juices. Choose early, mid and late fruiting varieties to stagger not just your fruit harvest but also the nectar rich flowers so that the local pollinators can sup from the delicate nectar rich flowers for longer.

Blueberries (*Vaccinium spp*)

Apart from being hailed as a super food rich in antioxidants and vitamins, the humble blueberry is also a top pollinator plant. It even has its own bumblebee species that feeds and specialises on its drooping flowers. The Bilberry bee, though rare and more localised to the northern parts of the UK, feeds predominantly on wild bilberries, a close relative of the cultivated forms.

Blueberries are one of the best choices of fruit to grow in pots, for several reasons. They are a bit fussy on the soil that they grow in, preferring acidic compost for the best results, which is easy to provide in a large planter. One established a plant can provide a generous crop of blueberries over the course of a few weeks, a handful a day on your cereal or yoghurt, and they really taste amazing picked straight off the plant.

The blueberry is the perfect fast food outlet for bumblebees and other pollinators and once you've got a trio of plants growing they will be buzzing with pollinators all summer. The fruit ripens in stages, rarely all at once, so you can keep picking the fruit and it means there are usually some flowers still there for the foraging pollinators too.

Blackberries (*Rubus fruticosus*)

Isn't funny how one group of plants can be regarded both as a garden thug and as a fruit bearing cane? Yes blackberries are vigorous plants, but not only can they bear simply delicious fat berries that are great in smoothies, desserts, juices and jams, but they are a fantastic food plant for pollinators. The blackberry (bramble) flowers are rich in nectar and are a vital food source in early and mid to late summer. The sugar rich nectar coincides with the peak foraging of pollinators, attracting all manner of bumblebees, solitary bees, hoverflies and butterflies. The plants are often self fertile, but the fruit that forms from cross-pollination is of a better quality and in much higher quantities than if the plants are left to self-pollinate. The decaying fruit is attractive to moths, wasps, butterflies and wild birds, so leave some fruit to mature on the plants. It is a larval food plant of the Green Hairstreak butterfly. Some solitary bees may nest in the hollow stems.

If you want a good crop it's best to choose a cultivated blackberry rather than try to tame and train the wild bramble. You can grow named varieties from fruit suppliers or garden centres that have been bred for taste and yield, and these will still be excellent forage plants for bees. And there are some thornless varieties so you can pick your fruit safely, feed the pollinators and have blackberry crumble or blackberry gin. Good thornless cultivars include 'Loch Ness' and 'Oregon Thornless'.

Recent research from the Botanic Garden of Wales (Ref 93) has shown that bramble flowers are the first choice for hoverflies and also many solitary bees.

If your garden borders the countryside or is delineated by mixed hedgerows you can also hide a bramble or two within the boundary, where its prickly stems can deter intruders, and where they weave their way through the thicket, offering nectar and pollen rich flowers for the insects and fruit for other wildlife.

Apples and Pears (*Malus and Pyrus spp*)

When I first started growing apples and pears in my garden I was rather surprised how few honeybees and bumblebees seemed to visit them. It was one of my first lessons about bees: if there's a better food source nearby the bees will be there. So if your trees are still establishing and blossom isn't abundant the local bees are more likely to visit the local cherry trees, especially the early flowering cherry plum where

Solitary bees such as this Andrena nitida are important pollinators of fruit trees. © *Jean Vernon.*

the food is more plentiful. That said, what I have noticed is that apples and pears are far more popular with some of the solitary bees, and in fact many solitary bees are better pollinators than the social bees. It's an important reminder that if you have an orchard, putting a hive of honeybees there doesn't necessarily ensure a good crop of fruit. It is just as important to provide nesting sites, forage and shelter for wild bees and our other pollinators that may choose to live nearby and that offer better quality pollination.

Plums and Cherries (*Prunus spp*)

The stone fruit family, which includes plums, cherries, apricots, peaches and nectarines, are some of the best fruit trees to grow for pollinators. They are rich in nectar and often flower quite early. If you've got large garden and love plums then you just can't beat a Victoria plum tree and you'll be rich in jams and jellies and juices forever. If you've got a hedge then plant the cherry plum. The very rare Black Hairstreak butterfly uses cherry species as a larval food plant.

One of the most important groups of plants for early spring pollinator blossom are the plums. © Jean Vernon.

FABULOUS FLOWERING SHRUBS

The great thing about flowering shrubs is that they last for decades and get better year after year. Ongoing research at the University of Bristol has measured nectar levels in hundreds of garden plants (Ref 88). Researchers found that shrubs are extremely good plants for pollinators because they provide so many flowers in one place. One flowering currant with 3,000 flowers provides as much nectar as 16,000 primrose flowers or 69,000 snowdrops. Shrubs like mahonia, hebe, lavender, berberis, pieris, ceanothus and pyracantha can be similarly rich. So a single shrub becomes a powerful hotspot or diner helping to support the pollinators on our doorsteps.

Currants for Bees (*Ribes spp*)

If you have borders in your garden where you can plant a few shrubs, it's a great way to introduce low maintenance, permanent structure to your borders and provide plant cafés specialising in pollen and nectar. One established shrub covered in flowers offers a great filling station for our pollinating friends and it's a great place to stake out to see the insect activity in your garden. On my plot there are a few shrubs that flower early, offering a rich source of nectar. One of the best is the flowering currant.

A medium sized bush will be covered in clusters of flowers, each cluster arranged like a bunch of grapes hanging from the stems. Stake it out and see what pollinators visit. The short tubular flowers are accessible for most pollinators, though some of the longer-tongued species may avoid. In my garden it is particularly popular with queens of the Early bumblebee. It is also a larval food plant of the Comma butterfly.

There is also a fabulous species with fuchsia-like red flowers that dangle from horizontal stems. It's great for growing against a wall and is another great bumblebee magnet. It's called *Ribes speciosum* and is sometimes known as the fuchsia flowering gooseberry and is definitely one to look out for.

Flowering currant (Ribes spp) is in flower as the bees are becoming active in spring. © Jean Vernon.

The Butterfly Bush (*Buddleia davidii*)

Read any article about attracting bees and butterflies to your garden and fairly high on the list is the butterfly bush. It's not called the butterfly bush for nothing, but it could equally be called the pollinator bar or the bee feeder, because it not only smells very sweet, almost honey like, but it has lots of tiny individual flowers in large clusters that are very rich in nectar. That means, once they've found a buddleia in flower the pollinators don't have far to go to collect a decent amount of sucrose rich fuel; it's all in one place and so they can feed and use less energy to do so.

In summer the fabulous flower spikes of these easy to grow plants are alive with nectar supping insects, especially bees, hoverflies and butterflies. On warm sunny days the gentle buzz of insects and the soft closing and opening of butterfly wings brings these plants alive. Take a closer look and you will see that it is actually only the longer-tongued pollinators that can feed here; the tiny individual tubular flowers are quite deep, holding the nectar at some depth for the pollinator to reach into the

The nectar rich flowers of buddleia are a magnet for butterflies like this Comma. © Martin Mulchinock.

flowers. That means short-tongued bees, wasps, flies and hoverflies will struggle, but that it's perfect for many of the longer-tongued beautiful summer butterflies such as Peacocks, Tortoiseshell, Comma and Red Admirals and some bumbles.

Plant breeders have been hybridising buddleias over the last few decades to create smaller, more compact varieties suitable for smaller gardens and even for growing in containers. Some of these plants are sterile, so they don't produce seed and won't cause a problem self-seeding in unwanted places. Many of them have nectar rich flowers. The spectacular Mullein moth caterpillar sometimes feeds on buddleia leaves.

There are dozens of fabulous varieties, and an NCCPG national collection at Longstock Park Nursery near Southampton (Ref 89) is a great place to visit to see them all in flower.

'Black Knight' which carries the RHS AGM, is a deep purple variety with a rich orange centre to each individual flower, and is a great choice. Plants grow to about 4m and are a magnet for butterflies and bees, especially Red Admirals and Peacocks.

Orange Ball Buddleia (*Buddleia globosa*)

This is quite a large sprawling shrub (can grow up to 4–8 metres) unless you keep it pruned and in check, but it flowers a bit earlier than 'normal' buddleia and has bright, glowing slightly scented orange balls of nectar rich flowers at the ends of the stems in late spring. There is a lemon yellow variety of this plant called 'Lemon Ball'. Prune back hard immediately after flowering.

The orange ball buddleia has bright orange marble like flowers rich in nectar. © Jean Vernon.

Buddleia x weyeriana flowers later and into autumn so it's great for late flying pollinators. © *Martin Mulchinock.*

Buddleia weyeriana 'Sungold' is a great late summer species, flowering well into autumn with its orange yellow plumes of nectar rich flowers. It will keep flowering right up to the first frost and in a mild winter can produce further richly scented flowers to feed winter emerging bees, butterflies and other pollinators on the wing.

BORDER CONTROL

In some places buddleia is regarded as a weed because it self-seeds quite readily and colonises barren soil and odd places including railway embankments and cracks and crevices in buildings and walls and even sometimes house gutters. It has become such a menace in some areas that it has been classified as an invasive plant. But there are ways to keep it under control. If you do grow it and your garden borders the countryside or a special wildlife site, then it's a good idea to remove the seed heads to stop the self-seedlings taking over precious habitat. The good thing about deadheading the flowers is that your plants will make more flowers, because buddleias flower on this year's stems. So you extend its period of flowering a little and increase the feeding opportunity for pollinators.

Oregon Grape (*Mahonia aquifolium*)

There are a few species and varieties of Mahonia that will flower in the winter garden. If you plant a few of these fabulous evergreen shrubs and choose some of the different variations you can create a winter nectar bar for pollinators. Mahonia are easy to grow and pretty low maintenance. Plant at the back of a border and give them space to establish; they will grow into a majestic shrub, flowering when few other things are in bloom and become a beacon for pollinators on the wing in the depths of winter.

Mahonia x media 'Charity' and other cultivars are the earliest to flower, in early winter, providing late season sustenance for pollinators. There is even a very aptly named and scented variety called 'Winter Sun' a perfect name for a diner where sugar rich nectar is on the specials' board for the duration of the flowers. The flowers of these Mahonias are borne *en masse* in spears of bright yellow in mid winter.

The scented *Mahonia japonica* is another great garden plant; flowering a little later with lemon yellow flowers followed by purple fruits that will feed the birds too. And then there's *Mahonia aquifolium*, a more straggly form, that spreads and suckers, but is just as good for pollinators, bearing dense clusters of rich yellow flowers in later winter/early spring. The variety 'Apollo' is a good choice as it is a more compact plant. This is the true Oregon grape and the fruits that form are edible, providing an interesting crop for the table, or you can leave them for the wildlife as a vital source of food for the birds.

In late winter the yellow flowers of mahonia are a great source of nectar and pollen for pollinators. © Debi Holland.

Winter Flowering Honeysuckle (*Lonicera fragrantissima*)

This is another garden shrub, ideal for the back of a border. It's a deciduous plant, so in winter it has bare stems where it forms flower buds that open to creamy white drooping flowers with exposed stamens providing easy access for pollinators. It's highly scented and flowers intermittently throughout the winter months depending on the weather. It's in the same plant genus (group) as the climbing honeysuckles, but this is a bushy shrub. Once it's finished flowering, it becomes clothed in mid green leaves and is pretty unassuming. Its winter flowers are a lifesaver for winter active pollinators, making it an essential choice for your pollinator garden.

Jacqueline Postill (*Daphne bholua*)

There are several forms of Daphne that you could grow as shrubs for winter pollinators but this one ticks all the boxes. It has scented, nectar-rich flowers that start to blossom as the first pollinators begin to stir and queen bumblebees emerge. It's good for many early pollinators like hoverflies, butterflies and moths, but it is poisonous if eaten by pets, wildlife, livestock and humans, so take care. It flowers as early as January or February with highly fragrant blooms in shades of soft pink. It's a slow growing shrub that you could grow in a large container. Plant it beside a garden seat or near the door so that you can appreciate its heady scent.

TREES FOR POLLINATORS

Trees with thousands of flowers in one place make gathering nectar and pollen more efficient and this is especially important for conserving vital energy when insects are collecting food. This makes trees a very important food resource for all sorts of garden pollinators. Even a small garden can have trees in large containers full of blossom and the trees can be under planted around their stems with other flowering plants and early spring flowering bulbs. Some trees, such as apples and pears, can be trained against a wall making good use of these vertical surfaces.

Most trees flower in spring and half a dozen, carefully chosen, different trees will provide precious pollen and nectar for garden pollinators. And of course the bigger the tree the more flowers it will produce. Alder, willow and hazel provide early pollen when food is scarce. Apple, quince, almond, plum, horse chestnut and single flowered cherry provide later sustenance.

Even the wild ivy that clambers up the trees provides essential autumn pollinator food. After centuries of study, mankind has only a basic understanding of this intricate relationship between insects and trees.

Some of these trees play a huge part in pollinator survival when the queen bumblebees and other insects emerge in spring. Willow trees with fluffy catkins loaded with yellow pollen attract bumblebees and hoverflies collecting protein rich pollen grains to nurture their young. In January and February willows may be one of the only sources of spring pollen.

Early flowering wild cherry trees have nectar rich flowers that pollinators will plunder for energy. Single flowered varieties allow easier access to the nectaries. Though beautiful, the decorative cherries with their fluffy, fairy-like pink candy floss flowers that we see in urban gardens and street plantings are of little use to our pollinating friends; the double flowers have often compromised the structure of the flowers so that there is no pollen or nectar. That's why many of the ornamental cherries don't actually produce any fruit. Instead, grow the real fruiting cherries for your own crop of plump cherries, which will also feed some of your garden pollinators, or choose the cherry plum for early nectar rich flowers and fruit for you and the wildlife.

Willow (*Salix spp*)

You might not think that willow trees flower, but it is the fluffy catkins that are the flowers, bearing either male or female parts on separate trees. It is the male trees where the silky grey catkins turn yellow with pollen in early spring and become a pop-up diner for our pollinators. The timing is just perfect for the queen bumblebees and hoverflies emerging in the sunshine. They need pollen to mature the eggs developing in their ovaries and the willow pollen is abundant. But the early emerging female solitary bees will also gather the pollen, eating some to mature their eggs and using the rest to provision their nests with food for their young. Willow trees, like many trees that bear catkins are normally wind-pollinated. The copious pollen is carried on the wind to nearby female flowers, equipped with sticky stigmas to catch the grains. But the flowers can also produce nectar, making them a vital food resource for pollinators of all types including early emerging butterflies.

Willows come in all shapes and sizes. Be wary of planting a real weeping willow in your garden, as these can reach a tremendous size and have been known to cause damage to underground structures. Look out for coloured stemmed willows that can be kept in check by hard pruning; this in turn encourages fresh, colourful stem growth. You can even buy standard willows with drooping stems (Kilmarnock willows) to grow in pots if space is an issue. Willows are important caterpillar plants for many moths, especially hawk moths and the Buff-tip moth as well as several species of woodland butterflies.

ATTRACTING GARDEN POLLINATORS

Hazel (*Corylus avellana*)

Hazel trees are amazing in spring and are also a very useful hedging plant, providing a crop of hazelnuts in the autumn for pesto and other seasonal menus for us and a source of pollen for garden pollinators. Hazel is also a caterpillar food plant for several butterfly and moth species. Allowed to grow unchecked the hazel will quickly reach tree proportions, but if you coppice (cut to the ground) the stems they will generate a crop of tall upright stems that will mature into pea sticks and bean canes for the

garden. Hazel is wind-pollinated and to ensure good pollination it makes a lot of rich yellow pollen-bearing catkins. The tiny female flower parts are red sticky stigmas formed close to the stems that trap the pollen grains blown onto them in the breeze. Hazel doesn't produce nectar, so the only pollinators you will find partaking in its pollen bounty are the females of the species that need this protein rich food source to develop their maturing eggs and feed their young.

For a really dramatic type of hazel for your garden consider the contorted form, known as the corkscrew hazel, which has an astounding growth habit that causes it to grow in an almost corkscrew pattern. These have a fabulous winter silhouette especially in the frost or snow. They don't grow as big as a normal hazel and they still produce catkins and nuts, making them an interesting choice for your garden.

The contorted hazel has lovely corkscrew stems, but still offers pollen-laden catkins. © Martin Mulchinock.

Alder (*Alnus glutinosa* and *Alnus viridis*)

It's a shame that alders aren't more widely grown as they can make very interesting plants for large gardens. They are particularly good for damp, boggy land and are great trees for wildlife. With early catkins bearing rich pollen and resinous buds, they attract garden pollinators and can be used as a screen or a windbreak. Better suited to large gardens, the trees are wind-pollinated and produce pollen rich catkins in January and February.

Horse Chestnut (*Aesculus hippocastanum*)

If you loved playing conkers as a child you might not realise what a beautiful flower the horse chestnut tree has, or that the sticky buds are a useful source of resin for a variety of different bees.

The spires of creamy white or pink flowers are rich in nectar and are an excellent food plant for pollinators. These grow to be very large trees so don't plant them in a small garden. If you have the space you can grow them from a conker, a great project with the kids, and then watch your sapling mature into a young tree.

The flowers on one established conker tree can provide copious nectar for insects. © Jean Vernon.

Winter Cherry (*Prunus x Subhirtella 'Autumnalis*)

Cherry trees are great pollinator plants as long as you choose the single flowered varieties. Most start flowering from spring onwards but there are a few that actually flower over the autumn and winter, providing an oasis of nectar rich flowers for any pollinators on the wing.

Despite the confusing name, *Prunus x subhirtella 'Autumnalis* flowers in winter, anytime from November to the end of February and sometimes into March, so it's not really autumnal at all. Sometimes it flowers in flushes, especially when a cold snap holds the buds tight, but these little winter jewels not only light up the garden but also provide essential nectar for winter active pollinators. Grow it as a small to medium tree within a mixed border. It won't cast much shade as it has an open habit and it even has attractive autumn hues at the end of the season.

Look out for white pollen dusted, ghost-like pollinators in late summer, it's a sign that Himalayan balsalm grows near. © Jean Vernon.

ATTRACTING GARDEN POLLINATORS

might find it growing in vast swaths along riverbanks and in damp ditches. And on closer observation you will notice a few things. First it has masses of flowers and these are very, very attractive to pollinators and particularly bees. The pollen and nectar are high grade and especially nutritious for our bee buddies. But perhaps the most fascinating thing about this plant is its seed dispersal mechanism, which incidentally is where it gets its botanical name. These plants are impatient to release their seed. The attractive rugby ball shaped seed pods explode with some force at the slightest touch, propelling the seeds far and wide and spreading the plants further into the landscape. You can actually hear the pods popping. The seeds aren't long lived, around 18 months, and the plants are annuals, dying back for winter and germinating from fresh seed in spring. This means that they can be controlled by removing the early spring growth or by preventing them from going to seed, which would require the flowers being removed before seed sets. A mammoth task for a large patch, but not impossible in a garden setting. I'm not suggesting that you grow it, but perhaps view it with rose-tinted spectacles where it does occur.

The Carrot Family (*Apiaceae spp*)

The members of the carrot family, more formally known as umbellifers or now apiaceae are rich in nectar making them great food plants. That includes some of our herbs like fennel, dill and lovage and some vegetables including carrots and parsnips. And some beautiful garden plants like *Ammi majus*.

Wild carrot flowers are beloved by pollinators. © Jean Vernon.

But there are some pretty poisonous members of this plant group, including hemlock water dropwort and hogweed, which you don't want in your garden, but that do grow on wasteland and beside rivers and streams.

From a pollinator perspective these plants make good landing pads and are sometimes used as living umbrellas to shelter them from the rain. The flat flower heads are a mass of tiny flowers over a small area, presenting a fast feeding site for these tiny insects. I'm not suggesting that you plant anything other than the edible and ornamental types, but just be aware that what is poisonous and deadly to us can also be a lifesaver for pollinators. Hoverflies and other flies as well as beetles, solitary bees and wasps are attracted to many of the apiaceae flowers.

Ragwort (*Senecio jacobaea*)

Ragwort is a really, really bad plant. Or so we are led to believe. But what if I told you that at least 30 insect species rely entirely on this plant for their survival and that 10 of those are rare? It's a food plant for 75 species of insects. Not only that but over 100 of our precious pollinator species feed on the rich nectar that the ragwort flowers produce. Without ragwort dozens of species of insects would cease to exist. Virtually all the tiger moth caterpillars eat it. The caterpillars of the cinnabar moth, which actually naturally control ragwort, are dependent on it.

Of course it is a danger to livestock if eaten fresh in the field, but it tastes really horrible and most herbivores avoid it, unless there is nothing else to eat. The biggest

Ragwort is poisonous to livestock, but an essential food plant for many wild species of insects, such as this clouded yellow butterfly. © Lance Featherstone.

problem is when the meadow is cut and the dried hay or silage contains ragwort, then it becomes more difficult to detect and will poison livestock if it is fed to them. But away from horses and livestock the presence of ragwort is considered to be important as a nectar source for pollinators and a host plant for a number of rare invertebrates that cannot feed on anything else. It is also a native UK plant and where it grows on uncultivated land and is doing no harm, could, perhaps, be allowed to grow (Ref 95).

WEEDS FOR BEES

It's not like me to call any plants a weed because quite honestly pretty much all the 'weeds' that flower are actually forms of wildflowers and most if not all of them are important in different ways for pollinators. Don't get me started on butterfly host plants, the plants that caterpillars eat before they pupate into the beautiful fairytale butterflies in our gardens. That's a whole book in itself, but it is worth remembering that most plants form the base layer and are important in the food chain. It's time we found out about some of these plants before we relegated them to the weed pile. It's far more efficient working with nature than trying to battle against her.

The really good thing about these wild plants is that they are not only survivors, growing easily in any bare soil, but that they will seed and spread themselves easily, so extending the forage for our precious pollinators. Of course there are places where we don't want them to grow, but most can be removed as seedlings or dug out as mature plants. If you don't want them to seed around your garden remove the fading flowers after they have supplied your pollinators with the pollen and nectar and before they set seed. But do bear in mind that some creatures, especially seed eating birds feast on the seeds of these so-called weeds.

Dandelion (*Taraxacum officinale*)

Don't reach for the weed killer when you see dandelions. These bright, cheery spring flowers are a vital pollen and nectar source for all types of bees and garden pollinators.

If ever there was a plant that needed re-evaluating it has to be the dandelion. Far from being a garden pest that many regard it as, this humble plant is rich in virtuous benefits. To some it's a pernicious weed and yet this, pretty, early spring flowering plant is a vital food source for pollinators and much more. The dandelion is the number one, early season, spring flower for pollinators. Let it grow.

Each one of the golden yellow flowers is a mass of a hundred or more individual florets, rich in high-energy nectar and pollen at a time when little else is in flower. Pollinators live on the knife-edge at this time of year. By the end of winter and start

In early spring, sometimes the dandelions are the only reliable source of pollen and nectar for pollinators on the wing. © Jean Vernon.

of spring, newly emerged creatures such as bumblebees, hoverflies and solitary bees need nectar fast to sustain their nest building activities. Pollen is high in protein and the perfect food for pollinators and yet with one swift sweep of the lawnmower we cut this precious food source weekly and deprive nature's army of pollinators of natural food. Several of our moth species use dandelions as a food for their caterpillar stage.

Dandelion has historically been used to stimulate the appetite. It can also be eaten, but it's essential to check with your doctor or pharmacist if you are taking any medicines that might interfere or interact with the herb. While dandelions are generally considered to be safe, some people can have an allergic reaction. So always exercise caution.

If you've checked and you are OK to eat them then you can utilise the young leaves as vital spring greens in salads (blanche them first under roofing tiles to dispel a little more of the bitterness), or feed the leafy wonders to pets (rabbits, guinea pigs and hens adore the leaves). Each one is packed full of vitamins, essential minerals and antioxidants. These productive plants are a perfect salad crop producing masses of cut and come again leaves and revered by top chefs for their ultra expensive menus. You can even steam them or cook them like spinach.

ATTRACTING GARDEN POLLINATORS

The flowers can be used to make dandelion wine and the roots roasted and dried to create a caffeine-free, coffee alternative.

If you have to control its spread then dig up the offending plants individually. Pick the flowers or remove them when they start to go over to prevent them from setting seed, or collect the seed heads in a muslin bag and distribute them elsewhere for the birds to eat.

Thistle (*Cirsium/Carduus/Carlina ssp*)

There are lots of different sorts of thistle, from the ones you might see growing on wasteland and farmers fields to a huge variety that plant lovers choose and plant in their gardens. They don't all have the prickly leaves we associate with these plants and the prickles themselves are a defensive mechanism that the plants have evolved to stop them from being eaten. They mostly belong to the same family, the asteracea, which are often good pollinators' food plants. Thistles are the larval food plant of choice for the Painted Lady butterfly. Goldfinches also feed on thistle seed heads.

Within the thistle group are plants such as cardoons and artichokes, which have extraordinary large flower heads.

The creeping thistle is regarded as a thug in gardens and fields and affects uncultivated soil, spreading by lateral roots growing underground, or indeed by its fluffy seeds. Nevertheless this weed has nectar and pollen rich flowers that are a magnet for pollinators. I am not suggesting that you grow it because there are many more garden worthy thistles to choose, but if it's growing in a patch where it can be left to flower and it's doing no harm, then leave it for the pollinators. If you do have to clear thistles from your ground, then do it manually without chemicals. The roots are brittle and will reroot if broken from the main plant (this is how it creeps) so be prepared to dig

Not all thistles are prickly thugs: knapweeds (Centaurea spp) are rich in nectar. © Jean Vernon.

over the ground for two or three seasons and please provide something else for the local pollinators to eat.

Why not choose a garden worthy member of this group of plants? Globe artichokes, if allowed to flower, will provide masses of pollen and nectar for pollinators in summer and you can eat the young flower buds too. Or grow some of the knapweeds, great for wildflower patches, or the blue-balled flower echinops, which bears a pompom full of flower heads that attracts a myriad of pollinators.

Vetch (*Vicia spp*)

Vetches in general are really good plants for pollinators, mostly offering a rich source of nectar. There are around 100 different flowering forms of vetch and many grow wild in our gardens and in the wider landscape. They are all part of the legume family and related to peas and beans. These plants are exceptional because they make their own nitrates in nodules on their roots and in effect feed themselves, and they also feed the soil. It's a big group of plants, but the ones that tend to be labelled as weeds are the wood vetch, hairy vetch and the cow vetch which is grown as a fodder crop and a green manure and has spread into gardens. But these plants are important food plants for pollinators, and especially the long-tongued bumblebees and moths that can reach into the flowers for the nectar.

Vetches can crowd out garden plants, but in a cottage garden setting they create useful filler in between the plants, with attractive purple flowers. As long as they are kept under control, and not allowed to take over, the vetches offer an attractive source of food for garden pollinators.

Some of the vetches and other members of the pea family are important larval plants for butterfly and moth caterpillars. For example, Kidney Vetch is a larval plant for the Small Blue Butterfly.

Teasel (*Dipsacus sativus*)

The pretty teasel is a tall prickly plant growing to several feet tall and topped with hedgehogesque spiky flower heads. They grow on wasteland, on road verges and along the margins of fields and are fairly common in the UK. The flower heads are fascinating, rings of soft mauve florets open up in circles up and down the prickly cone like head attracting a variety of nectar supping pollinators. It's a vital source of both pollen and nectar and also a larval food plant for some moth species and the Marsh Fritillary butterfly.

ATTRACTING GARDEN POLLINATORS

When the seed sets the plants become food for seed-eating birds such as goldfinches. You can dry and spray the spent seed heads for decoration or leave them in the garden for overwintering insects and birds. The plants spread via seed and are easy to grow from seed but they are biennial which means they germinate and grow in the first year and then grow and flower, set seed and die in the second year.

Teasels are important wildlife plants, with nectar rich flowers for pollinators like this Tortoiseshell butterfly and edible seeds for the birds. © Jean Vernon.

Learning More

The more you learn about pollinators and insects the more you realise how much more there is to learn. There are some fabulous books to read and lots of fascinating scientific papers and amazing websites.

Here are just a few that you might find interesting, but there are so many more. So this is just to get you started.

- *Dancing with Bees*, Brigit Strawbridge-Howard, Chelsea Green Publishing.
- *The Living Jigsaw*, Val Bourne, Royal Botanic Gardens, Kew.
- *Pollinators and Pollination*, Jeff Ollerton, Pelagic Publishing.
- *The Forgotten Pollinators*, Stephen L. Buchmann and Gary Paul Nabhan.
- Stephen Falk Flickr Site on Flickr.com
- *The Garden Jungle*, Dave Goulson, Vintage Press.
- *The Secret Life of Flies*, Dr Erica McAlister, Natural History Museum.
- *Complete Guide to British Insects*, Michael Chinery, Collins.
- *Britain's Hoverflies*, Stuart Ball and Roger Morris, Princetown University Press.
- *Field Guide to the Bees of Great Britain and Ireland*, Steven Falk, British Wildlife Publishing Ltd, Bloomsbury Wildlife Guides.
- *Benton Solitary Bees*, Pelagic Publishing, Naturalists' Handbook 33.
- *New Naturalist Bumblebees*, Ted Benton, HarperCollins
- *RSPB spotlight bumblebees*, Richard Comont, Bloomsbury.
- *Bumblebees An Introduction*, Nikki Gammans, Dr Richard Comont, S. C. Morgan, Gill Perkins, Bumblebees Conservation Trust.
- *A Sting in the Tale*, Dave Goulson, Vintage Jonathan Cape Ltd.
- *The Humble-Bee: Its Life-history and How to Domesticate it, with Descriptions of All the British Species of Bombus and Psithyrus*, Frederick Sladen.
- *Field Guide to the Moths of Great Britain and Ireland*, Dr Paul Waring, Martin Townsend, Bloomsbury Wildlife.
- *British Moths*, Chris Manley, Bloomsbury Wildlife.
- *Britain's Butterflies*, David Newland, Robert Still et al, Princetown University Press.

ATTRACTING GARDEN POLLINATORS

References

1. Baldock et al (2019) 'A systems approach reveals urban pollinator hotspots and conservation opportunities' https://www.nature.com/articles/s41559-018-0769-y?fbclid=IwAR2VofPLOoTQa-jFETk1uNNrdmVPw2GsGX_MPiZ5OGFFF5TMKgElBp5twxQ

2. Nicholas Tew, Bristol Uni Phd, https://besjournals.onlinelibrary.wiley.com/doi/10.1111/1365-2745.13598

3. Jeff Ollerton, *Pollinators & Pollination*.

4. Rollings, R., Goulson, D. Quantifying the attractiveness of garden flowers for pollinators. *J Insect Conserv* **23**, 803–817 (2019). https://doi.org/10.1007/s10841-019-00177-3

5. Liam Olds/ Fuller RM (1987) Biological Conservation, 40: 281–300.

6. https://www.nature.com/articles/srep34499?WT.feed_name=subjects_evolution

7. https://doi.org/10.1007/s00359-017-1176-6

8. Charles Darwin, cats, mice, bumble bees and clover, Carreck, Norman; Beasley, Toby; Keynes, Randall. (2009). *Bee Craft*. 91. 4–6.

9. Charles Darwin, cats, mice, bumble bees and clover, Carreck, Norman; Beasley, Toby; Keynes, Randall. (2009). *Bee Craft*. 91. 4–6.

10. https://www.darwinproject.ac.uk/commentary/life-sciences/tale-two-bees

11. Pashalidou, F. G., Lambert, H., Peybernes, T., Mescher, M. C., De Moraes, C. M. (2020). Bumble Bees Damage Plant Leaves and Accelerate Flower Production When Pollen is Scarce. *Science*, 368: pp. 881–884.

12. https://www.nhm.ac.uk/discover/what-do-wasps-do.html

13. http://www.brc.ac.uk/irecord/enter-non-native-records

14. https://www.nationalinsectweek.co.uk/discover-insects/bees-ants-wasps/ruby-tailed-wasps

15. Entomological communications – https://entomologicalcommunications.org/index.php/entcom/article/view/ec01006

16. Jeff Ollerton wordpress – Identifying British ichneumonid wasps: https://jeffollerton.wordpress.com/2016/08/17/identifying-british-ichneumonid-wasps-an-introductory-guide-from-the-nhm/

17. Nicola Prehn and Chris Raper, *Beginners Guide to identifying British ichneumonids*, NHM

18. Liam Olds.
19. Wikipedia – https://wiki.kidzsearch.com/wiki/Polydnavirus
20. Liam Olds.
21. https://www.researchgate.net/publication/326160699_Occurrence_and_biology_of_Pseudogonalos_hahnii_Spinola_1840_Hymenoptera_Trigonalidae_in_Fennoscandia_and_the_Baltic_states
22. *Pollinators & Pollination* Jeff Ollerton.
23. BTO – https://www.bto.org/understanding-birds/articles/blue-tit-diary
24. Butterfly Conservation – https://butterfly-conservation.org/butterflies/large-blue
25. Conversations/correspondence with Liam Olds.
26. Research by Dr Jeremy Thomas.
27. Conversations/correspondence with Mark Spencer.
28. Butterfly Conservation – https://butterfly-conservation.org/butterflies/holly-blue
29. UK Butterflies – https://www.ukbutterflies.co.uk/species.php?species=argiolus
30. UK butterflies – https://www.ukbutterflies.co.uk/species.php?species=cardui
31. WildlifeTrusts Butterflies without Borders – https://www.wildlifetrusts.org/butterflies-without-borders
32. https://butterfly-conservation.org/our-work/recording-and-monitoring/migrant-watch/painted-lady-2021
33. Conversation with Mark Spencer
34. UK Butterflies – https://www.ukbutterflies.co.uk/species.php?species=rhamni
35. University of Cambridge, Andrew Bladon – https://www.cam.ac.uk/stories/butterflies
36. https://butterfly-conservation.org/moths
37. https://butterfly-conservation.org/moths/why-moths-matter
38. Conversation with Mark Spencer.
39. https://butterfly-conservation.org/how-you-can-help/get involved/gardening/gardening-for-moths
40. www.butterfly-conservation.org
41. Butterfly Conservation – https://butterfly-conservation.org/moths/silver-y
42. Wildlife Trusts – https://www.wildlifetrusts.org/butterflies-without-borders
43. Jason Chapman et al.
44. Butterfly Conservation – https://butterfly-conservation.org/moths/mint-moth
45. https://www.sciencedaily.com/releases/2015/09/150901204819.htm
46. https://butterfly-conservation.org/our-work/recording-and-monitoring/migrant-watch/humming-bird-hawk-moth-2021
47. Conversation with Mark Spencer

48. Nat History Museum https://www.nhm.ac.uk/discover/toxic-talents-cyanide-moths.html

49. https://royalsocietypublishing.org/doi/10.1098/rsbl.2019.0877

50. Butterfly Conservation – https://butterfly-conservation.org/moths/buff-tip

51. Conversation with Mark Spencer.

52. ButterflyConservation – https://butterfly-conservation.org/moths/privet-hawk-moth

53. https://www.mothnight.info/

54. Conversation with Marc Carlton.

55. https://www.exeter.ac.uk/news/research/title_720384_en.html

56. *Britain's Hoverflies: An Introduction to the Hoverflies of Britain*, S. G. Ball, Roger Morris.

57. Stephen Falk Flickr Site – https://www.flickr.com/photos/63075200@N07/albums/72157629453425024/

58. Evidence for batesian mimicry in a polymorphic hoverfly Malcom Edmunds/Tom Reader https://onlinelibrary.wiley.com/doi/10.1111/evo.12308

59. https://www.stuff.co.nz/environment/wasp-wipeout/124271025/waspnest-beetle-and-hoverfly-get-epa-nod-for-war-on-wasps

60. RHS Advice – https://www.rhs.org.uk/advice/profile?pid=657

61. https://www.exeter.ac.uk/news/research/title_720384_en.html

62. *Britain's Hoverflies: An Introduction to the Hoverflies of Britain*, S. G. Ball, Roger Morris.

62A. Behavioural ecology https://academic.oup.com/beheco/article/27/6/1767/2453482?login=true

63. https://www.discoverwildlife.com/animal-facts/insects-invertebrates/bee-flies/

64. WLGF - http://www.wlgf.org/wildlife/bee_flies.html

65. Liam Olds

66. Bedfordshire Natural History Society – www.bnhs.co.uk

67. https://tachinidae.org.uk/blog/

68. https://www.britannica.com/animal/blow-fly-insect#ref270884

69. Jeremy Bartlett, Let it grow blog – https://www.jeremybartlett.co.uk/2018/03/16/cuckoo-pint-arum-maculatum/

70. https://www.sciencedirect.com/science/article/pii/S0005272808000881

71. 1991 paper 'The pollination of Arum maculatum L. – a historical review and new observations' by Lack and Diaz. *Watsonia* Volume 18, pages 337–342

72. https://www.buglife.org.uk/bugs/bug-directory/st-marks-fly/

73. Stephen Falk Flickr – https://www.flickr.com/photos/63075200@N07/collections/72157632177517531/

74. BugLife – https://www.buglife.org.uk/bugs/bug-directory/st-marks-fly/

75. BugLife – https://www.buglife.org.uk/bugs/bug-directory/st-marks-fly/

76. Dipterists Forum Flowers for Flies.

77. *Pollinators & Pollination* Jeff Ollerton.

78. https://www.nhm.ac.uk/discover/uk-beetles-british-most-spectacular-and-beautiful.html

79. NHM – https://www.nhm.ac.uk/discover/uk-beetles-british-most-spectacular-and-beautiful.html

80. RHS Advice

81. Torpor is the technical term applied to overwintering insects. They don't hibernate like a mammal but they do hunker down and shelter, often underground in a state resembling suspended animation.

82. Stephen Falk.

83. The aliens in the 1979 film *Alien* by Ridley Scott were inspired by the lifecycle of parasitoid insects.

84. http://nurturing-nature.co.uk/award-winning-solitary-bee-nesting-box/

85. http://www.rosybee.com

86. Bee Happy Plants is a great resource in the UK – www.beehappyplants.co.uk

87. There's a useful list of other nurseries and suppliers on the RHS Website – https://www.rhs.org.uk/advice/profile?pid=960

88. The importance of urban areas for flower-visiting insects – https://royalsocietypublishing.org/doi/10.1098/rspb.2014.2849

89. https://leckfordestate.co.uk/nursery

90. Dartmouth College. 'Parasitized bees are self-medicating in the wild' *ScienceDaily*, 1 September 2015. www.sciencedaily.com/releases/2015/09/150901204819.htm

91. Dartmouth College. 'Parasitized bees are self-medicating in the wild' *ScienceDaily*, 1 September 2015.

92. Nick Tew PhD student, Bristol University, *Quantifying floral resources for insect-pollinators in UK urban areas.*

93. Pollen DNA analysis research from National Botanic Garden of Wales. Natasha de Vere. Laura Jones, Georgina L. Brennan, Abigail Lowe, Simon Creer, Col R. Ford and Natasha de Vere (in press) 'Shifts in honeybee foraging reveal historical changes in floral resources', *Communications Biology.*

94. Pollen DNA analysis research from National Botanic Garden of Wales. Natasha de Vere. Laura Jones, Georgina L. Brennan, Abigail Lowe, Simon Creer, Col R. Ford and Natasha de Vere (in press) 'Shifts in honeybee foraging reveal historical changes in floral resources', *Communications Biology.*

95. https://www.buglife.org.uk/sites/default/files/Ragwort.pdf

Index

Scientific names for plants and insects are cross-referenced with common names. If you know the common name the scientific name should appear in brackets. If you know the scientific name the index should refer back to the common name.

ATTRACTING GARDEN POLLINATORS